Chrismukkah

OTHER WORKS BY GERSH KUNTZMAN

HAIR! Mankind's Historic Quest to End Baldness
(Random House, 2001)

SUV: The Musical!
(a play)

Hitler Would Have Double-Parked
(an unpublished novel)

Bad Seeds
(an unpublished novel)

Publish My Unpublished Novel
(an unpublished novel)

Chrismu

The
OFFICIAL GUIDE
to the
World's Most-Beloved
Holiday

Gersh Kuntzman

SASQUATCH BOOKS
SEATTLE

To Jane Marin Kuntzman,

who teaches me the valuable lesson

of Chrismukkah every day.

Printed in Canada
Published by Sasquatch Books
Distributed by Publishers Group West
15 14 13 12 11 10 09 08 07 06   9 8 7 6 5 4 3 2 1

Cover photograph: PhotoAlto

Cover and interior book design & composition:
Judith Stagnitto Abbate / Abbate Design

Interior illustrations: Richard Ewing

Library of Congress Cataloging-in-Publication Data is available.

ISBN 1-57061-489-X

Sasquatch Books
119 South Main Street, Suite 400
Seattle, WA 98104
(206) 467-4300
www.sasquatchbooks.com / custserv@sasquatchbooks.com

Contents

Introduction

A World of Chrismukkah

Goldstein: *What is this holiday you are celebrating,*
Horatio?
Horatio: *It is Chrismukkah, my lord.*
Goldstein: *How strange, yet how delightful.*
Horatio: *My lord, you have no idea.*

—**Shakespeare,** *A Chrismukkah's*
Tempest Tale, act 1, scene 4

ALL AROUND THE COUNTRY, Americans are celebrating Chrismukkah like never before. The Goldstein-Sanchezes of Millburn, Massachusetts, ring in the holiday by eating extra-salty potatoes on a large mound of dirt. The D'Allesandro-Weinbergs of Rapid City, South Dakota, mark the day by singing Chrismukkah carols to their neighbors and returning perfectly suitable presents. The Gifford-Halberstams of Miami, Florida, bring a twist to the Measuring of the Children—a Chrismukkah ritual since the 1300s—by placing the record of everyone's height in an envelope, mailing it to themselves, and not opening it until the next Chrismukkah, at which time they delight in comparing the new season's statistics with those from the year past. And Evan Tarnovsky-Jones of Hibbing, Minnesota, simply sits in a dark room and smokes hashish.

But who is celebrating Chrismukkah correctly? Why ho, ho, hold on a second: They *all* are!

Admittedly, I was always a skeptic of Chrismukkah, feeling that it was merely a fictitious celebration, a made-for-TV event to satisfy a critical demographic, a way for rootless Jews and recovering Christians to find some sort of uneasy middle ground between their somewhat more famous annual rites, a way for intermarried couples to ring in the season without having to buy a Christmas tree yet call it a "Hanukkah bush" or light a menorah but call it a "Christmas candelabra." It all seemed as fake as the baby Jesus in the White House crèche.

But my research for this book took me to places where Chrismukkah remains real and vibrant. In the Holy Land, I uncovered the long-lost roots of the holiday inside some urns that had been buried in a first-century garbage dump—and learned an uplifting tale of hot, forbidden, interfaith love. In Rome, archeologists allowed me to watch as they painstakingly unearthed the home of Sol Yutstein and Flavia Menses, the world's first intermarried couple, where I saw how one man risked his life to save Chrismukkah for all of us. In Minsk, the head of the Belarusan Theological Seminary allowed me unfettered access to records, notebooks, and transcripts that revealed how a half-dozen medieval rabbis interpreted, modernized, and, in some ways, obfuscated the Chrismukkah story that remains with us today. In Plymouth, Massachusetts, I found an addendum to the original passenger manifest of the *Mayflower*, discovering that there were four Chrismukkans aboard—and learned how they struggled to keep their faith, even as their fellow colonists held them up to Crueltie, Scorne, and the painfully superfluous insertion of the letter *e* in a variety of common nouns. In London, I got lost in the basement of the Charles Dickens Museum, opened a door that led into a dark room, stumbled forward, crashed through another door, and then fell through the rotted subbasement floorboards until I was face to face with Dickens's own handwritten notebooks—one of which contained the master's unpublished novella, *A Chrismukkah Carol*. At the headquarters of the Middleton Greeting Card Company in Davenport, Iowa, I was free to roam about as card artists and executives created—from scratch—the Middleton version of Chrismukkah—and learned that Chrismukkah has become such a vital part of our culture that companies are competing to see who can best exploit and cheapen it. In other words, is this a great country, or what?

And in home after home across America, I met hundreds of everyday people who shared with me the joy of Chrismukkah. And I learned that this holiday exists as surely as there is hallucinogenic greenery to burn, as certainly as there are monotone holiday songs to sing, as long as there are children to measure. Yes, Virginia Portnoy-Thomas, there *is* a Chrismukkah. So grab a sack of potatoes, buy some day-old bialys, return those unneeded gifts—and follow me, dear reader: It's Chrismukkah time!

But indulge me for a second: I would be remiss if I did not thank the many people who made this invaluable treasury possible, most notably Allen Salkin, who, after realizing he was too busy to write the book himself, mentioned several other authors to Sasquatch Books before getting around to recommending me. I'd also like to thank my wife, Julie Rosenberg, who, let's face it, has been putting up with a lot lately; the cast of *SUV: The Musical*; the entire staff of The Tea Lounge on Seventh Avenue in Brooklyn, who kept me caffeinated and inspired; David Shenk, with whom I have a reciprocal "acknowledgements" agreement; Eric Oleson, who deserves more than thanks, but I'm a little short on cash right now; Dana Youlin at Sasquatch Books for her fine editing; my lawyer, Kurt Hirsch, for working out an amazing royalty deal that apparently earns me royalties every time someone sings "Chrismukkah Is Coming to Town"; and Scott Campbell and his wife, Linda

Campbell, owners of @SQC. on New York's Upper West Side, who provided me with ample nourishment and the inspiration for the Chrismukkah recipes in Chapter 5 (recipes that the Campbells now serve every December, thanks to this project—hey, maybe they should be thanking *me*).

—**G. K.**

Brooklyn, September 2006

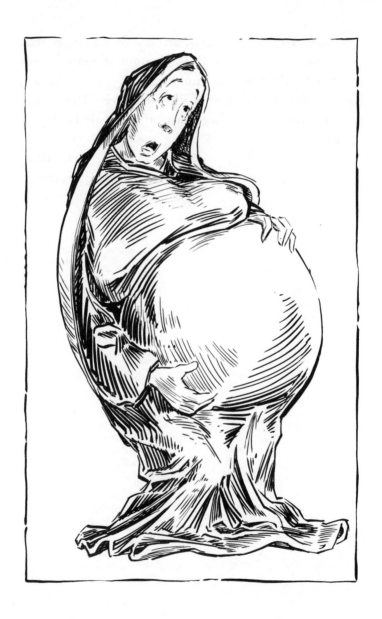

CHAPTER 1

The Origin of Chrismukkah

I sing of arms and of a man
Hardened in battle, but softened by a holiday.
It was Chrismukkah and it was celebrated from Troy to Sparta,
Its central ritual being the consumption of stale breadstuffs.
                    —Virgil, *The Aeneid*

BETHLEHEM, ISRAELI-OCCUPIED WEST BANK—This historic town has been welcoming pilgrims of all sorts for millennia. But I did not come here seeking the fabled manger where Jesus Christ entered the world or the tomb of the Jewish matriarch Rachel, but on another spiritual quest: the search for the epic roots of the world's most beloved holiday, Chrismukkah.

Although it is celebrated by nearly a billion people worldwide, the origins of the holiday have eluded historians and biblical scholars—and it might have eluded me as well. I had been researching Chrismukkah for nearly six years but had reached the limits of existing scholarship. My first two books on the subject, *In Search of Historic Chrismukkah* and *The Chrismukkah Story from Ramses to Roosevelt*, sold well, of course, but they had more holes in them than a paper bull's-eye at a police pistol range. I knew there was a story out there—the biblical story of the history of Chrismukkah—but scholars simply had not uncovered it yet.

Of course, I had a contract to write this book, so I prepared to do what I do best: crank out the same old story, sprinkled with whatever new material I could find. But as I sat down to write, I was lucky enough to get a call that changed my life, my editor's life, and, indeed, the lives of everyone reading this sentence. Archeologists digging near the walls of this fabled city had struck gold—or, more accurately, they'd struck garbage, which is about as close to gold as archeologists ever get. In an ancient trash pile near the center of town, they'd uncovered two large urns. The lead archeologist, Dr. Sydney Driscoll of the University of Smerdlosk in Russia, knew their significance and, aware of the depth of my interest in Chrismukkah, called me immediately. I was on a plane three hours after I got the call (I would have been on a plane sooner, but you know how the traffic is to JFK on weekdays).

Driscoll waited until I got to the dig before opening up the urns. For years, he and I had been seeking what is the Holy Grail of archeologists: the two missing books of the Bible, the Gospel of Zebulon and the Book of Rotations. They're both mentioned in various biblical-era texts—the Dead Sea Scrolls won't shut up about them!—and there are fakes at the Vatican library, but no one had ever found the originals. Finally, here I was, face to face (or, more accurately, nose to stench) with two urns that had spent the last two thousand years buried in a Bethlehem landfill, perfectly preserved for centuries under mounds of rotting papyrus, pressed olives, crushed grapes, and plague victims. Being under all that garbage for all those years didn't only preserve the contents of the urns in a climate-controlled bubble, it also kept them safe from centuries of bounty hunters who tend to focus their attention on archeological digs that will yield gold or jewels, not raw sewage or historic scrolls. Let's face it, the vast majority of biblical-era scrolls only contain dietary rules anyway.

Driscoll pried open the lid on the first urn and inserted cloth-covered tongs. Carefully, he removed the rolled-up document inside and gently flattened it against the velvet-topped work table. Lifting a photographer's loupe to his eye, he focused on a bit of scribbled writing in the margin.

"So *that's* where Jesus put Mary Magdalene's phone number!" Driscoll joked. Those archeologists. I'd been on at least six digs with Driscoll, and he always made the same joke.

My eyes hungrily scoured the document, looking for purchase. But I could find nothing recognizable.

"You don't read Sumerio-Zorao-Farsi?" Driscoll asked incredulously. He knew I was fluent in Arabic, Aramaic, Hebrew, Hebraic, English, and Englaic, so he just assumed

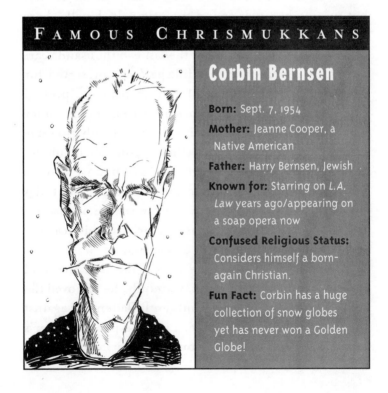

FAMOUS CHRISMUKKANS

Corbin Bernsen

Born: Sept. 7, 1954

Mother: Jeanne Cooper, a Native American

Father: Harry Bernsen, Jewish

Known for: Starring on *L.A. Law* years ago/appearing on a soap opera now

Confused Religious Status: Considers himself a born-again Christian.

Fun Fact: Corbin has a huge collection of snow globes yet has never won a Golden Globe!

I could read the ancient Chrismukkan language. But I didn't care if I couldn't read the actual scrolls. I'd come halfway around the world and I was staring at a document that would forever change mankind's understanding of its own history. So what if my publisher would have to hire a translator at $1,000 an hour? So what if we'd need at least 10,000 man-hours to get it done? I was about to change the world. I was about to learn the Chrismukkah story.

I Know Not What Myrrh Is: The Fourth Gift

B its and pieces of how Chrismukkah came into being could, of course, be gleaned from existing texts. The Gospel of Luke and the Gospel of Matthew mention Chrismukkah in passing, but both books spend an inordinate amount of time focusing on the birth of Jesus, which was, inarguably, a very important and widely anticipated event in the ancient world. Matthew explains that the event was so widely anticipated, in fact, that King Herod dispatched his sage scholars (the Wise Men) to Bethlehem, telling them, "Go and search diligently for the young child and when ye have found him, bring me word again, that I may come and worship with him also" (Matthew 2:8). It was a ruse, of course; Herod knew the prophecy that a new king would be born and wanted the Wise Men to smoke out the baby Jesus so that he could kill him before he took Herod's place on the throne. The story explains how the Wise Men waited outside Bethlehem until a star led them to the manger where the baby Jesus lay:

And when they were come into the house, they saw the young child with Mary his mother, and fell down, and worshipped him: and when they had opened their treasures, they presented unto him gifts: gold, and frankincense, and myrrh. (Matthew 2:11)

But thanks to Driscoll's discovery of the Gospel of Zebulon and the Book of Rotations, we now know that Matthew is not the final word on the subject. In fact, the very first reference to the Wise Men is in Zebulon, chapter 2, verse 3—and the passage makes clear that there were four, not three, Magi:

Herod summoned his four scholars and sent them forth from the East to await the birth of the child. Herod, not wanting to enrage the baby king of the Jews, instructed his scholars to bear four treasures, among them gold, and frankincense, and myrrh, and leave them at the child's feet.

And Zebulon contradicts Matthew in several other key ways, firstly, the amount of time the Wise Men had to wait on the outskirts of Bethlehem before the baby was born. Although Matthew makes it appear as if the baby Jesus were born right away, Zebulon is clear on the subject:

Mary, being several days past her date of predicted delivery, was greatly discomfited by the future king of the Jews, who did squirmeth at the most inconvenient of times, such as when Mary attempteth to sleep. The waiting was interminable for Mary, who at one point, did declareth, "Future king or not, I just want this thing out of my body already." The Wise Men waited patiently, observing a fast between meals. (Zebulon 2:8–10)

The Wise Men, equally distressed at the amount of time it was taking to produce the Lord, endured the wait by telling and embellishing old war stories:

The Magi told and retold the stories of their previous triumphs among themselves, succumbing to laughter even though they had heard the tales so many times before. But, alas, the travelers depleted even their stock of self-aggrandizing stories, and took up varied diversions, including whittling, expectorating at targets, and, eventually, measuring body parts and comparing the sizes with each other. Finally, they even went so far as to befriend several shepherds and nomadic tribesmen who had been drawn to the commotion of the impending birth of the Lord. (Zebulon 2:11–14)

Now, Rotations is fairly consistent on the subject of shepherds, giving the impression that a person would have to be extremely bored before even engaging one in conversation:

The shepherds were a smelly lot. To spend an hour with a shepherd, nay, to pass an evening with one, would be extremely displeasant. A shepherd could talk for hours about the condition of a sheep's fecal matter, for example, and cared little whether his listener was eating. And a shepherd would always inquire, "Are you going to finish that?" whenever a dinner guest had failed to return his attention to a piece of food within five minutes, no matter how lost in animated conversation he had become.   (Rotations 3:6)

But the Wise Men had passed the point of caring. They couldn't leave their encampment, lest the king of the Jews be born while they were out, so they invited the shepherds to pass the time with them. One of the shepherds, Ezekiel, told such a delightful story of an incident involving a wolf, an olive tree, and a mysterious whirlwind that the Wise Men offered to share some of their treasures with him and his fellow shepherds. But their offering did not go as planned:

"Not for nothing, but what use have I for gold, frankincense, and myrrh?" Ezekiel asked. "I know not even what myrrh is. Gold is useful only in the city, for the purchase of baubles for which I have no need. And you give me frankincense as if I am some stylist of women's hair! But, pray, what is this leafy substance in this yonder container? It appeareth that you sought to keep its contents entirely to yourselves."   (Zebulon 2:23–28)

Several books of the Bible make mention of the Wise Men's fourth gift for the baby Jesus, but there is hardly any consensus on what it was. Luke refers to it only as "sustenance," while Matthew calls it "nourishment." But Rotations is the most definitive:

The fourth gift, secreted inside a dried-out sheep stomach, was a substance grown in a valley east of the Dead Sea known only to the Magi, who cultivated their plantings with great patience and discretion. Once a week, one of the Magi would go into town and exchange a small portion of their crop for gold. Many customers would roast the entire plant, from the thick stem to the leaves, and consume it whole. King Herod was a particularly steady customer for the crop, but he would remove the leaves, stuff them into the many chambers of a menorah, ignite the dried leaves, and inhale deeply. The King said the smoke enabled him to envision great things for his people, although he bemoaned that he often lacked the motivation to actually realize these dreams. He would also bitterly complain that the royal cook rarely left enough food in the larder to nourish him after burning the leaf.   (Rotations 3:31–38)

Shamed, the Wise Men did share the fourth gift with the shepherds:

"Lo, let us divide up our crop among the shepherds and consumeth same," said the Wise Man Solomon. "If, of course, someone has stolen some fire from the gods." Everyone laughed at Solomon's sly reference to ancient Greek mythology.   (Zebulon 2:28–33)

A great cry of "Hallelujah" went up, and the leaves were divided between the Magi and the shepherds. A

Sean Penn

Born: Aug. 17, 1960

Mother: Eileen Ryan, devout Catholic

Father: Leo Penn, nonobservant Jew

Known for: Roles as a Hollywood bad boy—but with a moral code

Confused Religious Status: Has confessed to being an agnostic but was married to Madonna, who was once a Catholic but now practices Kaballah, a form of Jewish mysticism.

Fun Fact: Sean's grandparents ran a Jewish deli in New York City for years!

cloud of smoke filled the sky, drifting eastward and signaling to everyone in Bethlehem that while the baby Jesus was not yet born, there was much anticipatory rejoicing in the hills around town. The mystical herb induced intense discussions. Ezekiel, who was unaccustomed to the powerful smoke, claimed to see the face of Moses in a passing cloud. The Wise Man Solomon believed briefly that he had three hands. And the Wise Man Ben Ben-Rubin was so intoxicated that he started trash-talking Joseph.

"What's with this guy?" Ben-Rubin said, passing the burning herb roll to one of the shepherds. "His wife is great with another man's child and he doesn't seem to care! It's not alchemy to see that this guy is being played like a lyre!"   (Rotations 2:35–36)

In all, the Magi and the shepherds waited four days for the birth of the future Lord, consuming six goats, three sheep, eight skins of wine, and a sheep stomach of dried leaves. Such a quantity should only have been able to last one day, but it lasted the entire four—and it was not as if anyone had been rationing himself. Rotations provides the definitive account of what happened next, which closely matches Matthew, except for one or two very small details:

Alas, a star rose from the east and stopped directly over the Christ child. The Wise Men knew the time had come for them to rush from the hills and to lay their remaining gifts at the feet of the child in the manger. But before they left, they bade the shepherds good-bye and vowed to return to the encampment every year at the same time, with the same amount of dried leaves, to celebrate the brotherhood and fellowship they had shared with the shepherds, as well as the miracle of the self-replenishing sheep stomach. "We have witnessed a miracle," the Magi Solomon said. "I myself am so sated that I am even willing to believe that the son of God is actually lying in that manger downtown." "Wow," said one of his compatriots, "you are truly baked like a piece of unleavened bread in the Sinai."

(Rotations 3:21–28)

The remaining part of the biblical story—as far as the Wise Men are concerned—is, as we say, history. They laid their gifts at the feet of the baby Jesus and the world got Christianity in return. After that, the Wise Men got a little busy tending to their crop and their new religion, so it's no surprise that they failed to show up at the encampment as promised the next year. Or the year after. Or after that. In fact, the absence of the Wise Men became something of a running joke among the shepherds, who showed up at the campsite every year to continue the tradition. Eventually, of course, the shepherds gave up—they were Jews, after all, and had plenty of other holidays from which to choose. In protest to the growing Christian holiday of Christmas, the shepherds revived a fairly obscure holiday called Hanukkah and started celebrating it with vigor.

The First Fried Potato Stand
in the Holy Land

But, alas, the shepherds eventually fell on hard times. The ancient Israelites had only one primary source of fuel—the burning of donkey excrement—and overconsumption of this energy supply had thickened the skies over all of Judea from the Mediterranean to ancient Mesopotamia. The phenomenon was so bad that it is even mentioned in the Bible:

The thick clouds allowed sunlight to penetrate, but, alas, did not allow the heat from that very same sun to disperse back upward into the heavens. Over time, the temperature of the earth rose, like the conditions inside one of Aaron's greenhouses—a greenhouse effect, if you will. **(Rotations 6:24)**

Few citizens of the day gave much concern to the rising temperatures, preferring to simply dress in lighter-colored clothing, but the shepherds noticed the changes immediately. Long-standing watering grounds slowly dried up, and pastureland went fallow. Ezekiel himself, the hero of the fabled meeting with the Wise Men, had to sell his flock and move into the city, where, ironically, he got a job as a stylist of women's hair. Even after the rest of the family had relocated to Bethlehem, Ezekiel's grown daughter, Leah, remained at the site of the sacred meeting with the four Wise Men, eking out a meager living growing potatoes on a small plot. But she was miserably poor and sadly alone.

Meanwhile, in a valley on the eastern bank of the Dead Sea, things were also not so great. The drought had killed the Wise Men's highly lucrative crop and turned the nearby rivers and streams so brackish that the only source of revenue was the salt that they harvested from the Dead Sea itself. Every month, all four Wise Men would go forth from their valley into the cities to sell their harvest. King Herod was still a client, but he was not nearly as satisfied a customer. In fact, the King dedicated himself to finding alternative fuels so that the drought would end and the Wise Men could return to cultivating their original crop. Herod was so inspired, in fact, that he invented solar power—but the scheme failed when Herod failed to also invent something he called "batteries," which could store the energy of the sun's rays after the sun had set for the day.

One day the Wise Man Solomon was en route to his customers in Jerusalem when a true miracle occurred:

A great whirlwind blew sand and dust about, making it impossible for Solomon to see where he was going. His donkey had lost all sense of direction in the maelstrom, so Solomon decided to wait out the storm in a small ravine. Hours later, the storm did indeed pass, but Solomon had no idea where he was. And he was hungry, having nothing to consume but his own concoction of donkey milk, salt, and urine. Just as he felt he would never find his way again, he spied a woman tending her crops and made his way toward her. At first, he did not recognize her, nor she him. But something about his clothing, his bearing, and the small pipe he wore on a chain around his neck reminded her of someone.

"Solomon?" Leah asked.

"Leah, daughter of Ezekiel? Could it possibly be you?"

"It is I," Leah responded.

"Wow, great. Do you have anything to eat?"

Leah explained that all she had were her humble potatoes. But she offered them freely. "They taste bland and of the earth, but they are yours—if you will have them," she said.

"But, alas, Leah, I too have only a humble offering—the salt that I carry in my satchel to Jerusalem."

"Salt?" Leah said, somewhat crestfallen. "But didn't you once grow that great leafy herb?"

"The drought hath destroyed my crop and my livelihood—and even ruined my friendships, which I learned weren't based on friendship at all, but on my wondrous herb! I curse that plant! Where was I? Oh, yes, these bland potatoes. Well, let us spill my salt over thy potatoes and hope for a miracle."

(Rotations 5:22–48)

It wasn't a miracle, of course, but neither Leah nor Solomon could remember roasted potatoes that tasted so divine. Fully sated, Solomon pulled out his sextant and astrolabe in hopes of determining where he was. The results revealed the true miracle: Not only was he on the site of the sacred meeting between his fellow Wise Men and the shepherds, but also the positioning of the sun, moon, and stars was exactly the same as it had been on the night twelve years earlier when the shepherd Ezekiel turned down the gold, frankincense, and myrrh in favor of the hallucinogenic crop. In deference to the miracle, Solomon vowed to stay with Leah. The two merged their meager holdings and soon opened the first fried potato stand in all of the Holy Land. As word spread of the delicious fried potatoes, Leah and Solomon became rich beyond their wildest imaginations. Eventually, Solomon asked Leah to be his wife. She was not his ideal beauty, what with her Semitic nose and kinky hair, but she accepted, although she wasn't all that attracted to Solomon's dark complexion and distinctly Persian features. But they were in love.

Of course, the announcement of their impending marriage pleased neither Ezekiel nor the other Wise Men. "This is wrong, Leah," Ezekiel thundered. "Solomon is one of the Wise Men. His customs are strange to us and, need I remind you, his best friend is that Jesus character, who has given our people nothing but suffering and, I fear, will someday provide the philosophical underpinning for evildoers who would destroy us. Imagine that, killing Jews in the name of God! It's going to be ironic, I'll tell you that."

Meanwhile, the Wise Men were also counseling Solomon against the union. "Solomon, Leah is charming, yes, but she is a Jewess!" said one of the Wise Men. "If you marry her, you can say goodbye to roast pork,

Oliver Stone

Born: Sept. 15, 1946

Mother: Jacqueline, lapsed Catholic—and French, to boot!

Father: Lou Stone, nonobservant Jew—and a stockbroker, to boot!

Known for: Conspiratorial films/ fighting in the Vietnam War

Confused Religious Status: Stone converted to Buddhism, the golden retriever of religious denominations.

Fun Fact: Oliver's father took him to a prostitute to lose his virginity when he was in his midteens!

oysters, and oral copulation!" But Solomon was undeterred: "That's a myth! I know plenty of Jewish women who eat pork!"

There was some family tension after the wedding, especially toward the end of the year. Ezekiel expected Leah and her new husband to journey to Bethlehem every December to celebrate Hanukkah, an eight-day holiday that required the consumption of lots of greasy food to celebrate a supposedly miraculous supply of vegetable oil. Meanwhile, the Wise Men commanded Solomon to bring his new wife to their annual Christmas dinner, where they would be expected to show up with presents for everyone and enjoy a large meal of roast turkey, even though they had just had *the very same* meal a month earlier at The Giving of Thanks, a venerable harvest festival. Leah and Solomon were frustrated at all the traveling, especially given all the donkey carts they'd get stuck behind. But to defy one's family was even more difficult than stop-and-go traffic along the Jerusalem-Galilee tollway. At last, though, Leah and Solomon could take it no longer. "Five hours from Jerusalem to Bethlehem!" Solomon cried, when they had finally returned home from a day that required them to spend Hanukkah morning with Leah's parents and then have Christmas dinner with the Wise Men. "It's normally a 45-minute trip! That's it. This is the last time we do this. Next year, they're all coming to our place."

Fortunately, both clans agreed to meet at the sacred encampment to celebrate the union of their two families. Even more fortunately, the drought had ended, and the Wise Men were able to return to their original cultivation, which helped eliminate much of the tension at the gathering. The meal was humble, of course, as Solomon and Leah had created no shared rituals except the frying of the salty potatoes. But everyone got through it without any major family arguments, although Ezekiel, that provocateur, constantly tried to goad the Wise Men into political discussions: "What's with that Herod of yours? I'm paying taxes here and all we get are more temples and palaces!" But the Wise Men would not bite.

Leah and Solomon lived happily ever after, combining their disparate cultures and heritages into one, and casting aside old rituals in favor of new ones. As Rotations tells us,

In fact, Leah and Solomon felt so wealthy in their happiness that every year, to commemorate the first meeting of the Wise Men and the shepherds, they made an offering of fried potatoes to the poor and indigent. (Rotations 7:14)

It is here that the scrolls run out. "Isn't there more?" I asked Driscoll.

"Not unless you have $5 million for another dig," he said. "Problem is, there's nothing more in these two urns. We have found the Gospel of Zebulon and the Book of Rotations, but, alas, the long-lost Gospel of Ignatz eludes me!"

Bagelus Maximus:
Sol Yutstein and Flavia Menses

B ut I was satisfied and headed home, knowing that
there was enough raw material in the two newly discovered scrolls to keep me busy for years. Plus, I would
have to do several more years of additional research in
order to put the marriage of Solomon and Leah into
perspective. I needed to know, for example, why Solomon and Leah's call to create a new family celebration
remained unanswered for centuries. Clearly, it was time
for me to get out of the libraries and get back into the
field. I called Driscoll, who told me that he and a few
friends were freelancing on a dig in the center of Rome
that they hoped would unearth a first-century home
believed to contain details of the world's first intermarriage. Again, I was on a plane—two hours after getting stuck in gridlock on the Van Wyck Expressway, of
course.

On board, I brushed up on my knowledge of ancient
Rome, circa AD 64. Jesus Christ had been dead for
about 64 years, but the torch was being carried by believ-
ers throughout the empire. These bedraggled followers
were called "Christians," and the previous six decades
had not been great ones for them. Exercising their
cultlike beliefs in whatever secret place they could—in
underground catacombs, in stables, in the few hetero-
sexual bars of ancient Rome—they knew that, if caught

A Brief History of Jew/Non-Jew Holidays

History tells us there were many abortive attempts to bring together Jews and non-Jews in celebration before the earliest form of Chrismukkah shortly after the birth of Christ. In 643 BC, a group of rabbis sought out the Zoroastrian prophet, Zoroaster, in hopes of finding common ground for a joint harvest festival. But the rabbis abandoned the discussions after Zoroaster refused to abandon his faith's insistence on two hours of daily exercise. In 522 BC, the Judaean ambassador to the East, Abraham Zolowitz, met with the recently enlightened Buddha, Siddhartha Gautama. Zolowitz and Siddhartha agreed on the need for suffering to purify the soul, but the discussions broke down when Zolowitz steadfastly disagreed that *he* should be the one to suffer. And in 134 BC, Judaean naval officers lost at sea encountered three Shinto high priests on an island near present-day Hong Kong, and, after a filling meal of uncooked fish, they bonded over the fact that none of them believed in an afterlife. Still, the group failed to invent a new holiday after a disagreement over whether God was a living entity who created us or merely a small bonsai tree that happens to catch the light just right in the late afternoon.

by the Roman authorities, a date with a lion at the Colosseum awaited.

At the time, Jews were far more tolerated than Christians, yet the Jewish population of Rome knew that to hold on to its fragile place in the social order of daily life, Jews had to act like "normal" Romans by making daily sacrifices to Juno and the minor household gods, swearing fealty to the Emperor, and vomiting repeatedly after large meals. (For many Jews, this was not actually a sacrifice—specifically after a visit to their mother-in-laws' houses.) In fact, some Jews were even able to prosper during this period. One of the most prominent Jews of the era, Sol Yutstein, opened the Eternal City's first Jewish bakery, Senatus Populus Que Bagelus, and later struck it rich by introducing the pizza bagel. But history would remember him best for his participation in the world's first intermarriage—his union with the Christian Flavia Menses. (On second thought, Yutstein's greatest legacy is probably the pizza bagel. After all, some Jew would've married a Christian eventually, but the pizza bagel was a moment of true artistic inspiration.)

Little else was known of Yutstein, which was why I was so eager to join the dig. I got there just in time to help unearth what appeared to be a bedside table. We gently pried open the drawer and found a relic of unparalleled archeological value: The personal journals of both Sol Yutstein and Flavia Menses! (As a researcher, I constantly have to ask myself: Am I lucky or just so damn good?) The stories they would recount—the roots of their marriage, the trials of being the first inter-faith family, the inner struggle over why the pizza bialy never caught on—would no doubt provide an invaluable resource for me.

Driscoll put on a pair of chamois-covered gloves and delicately opened Yutstein's journal. Grabbing his photographer's loupe, he focused on a small bit of scribbling in the margins. "So *that's* where Brutus put Caesar's number!" he joked (and I laughed, pretending I hadn't heard the joke a million times). But then we got down to business reading the historically invaluable trove. Good thing I'm fluent in Ancient Latin.

Reading Sol Yutstein's journal, I learned that, as a Jew, he was tolerant of all Rome's ethnic minorities, including the Christian cultists who made up a small portion of his clientele. The way Yutstein saw it, people weren't "Jewish," "Christian," "Roman," "Gnostics," "Barbarians," or "Visigoths"—once they walked into his store, they were all bagel lovers. Yutstein loved all his customers, but there was one woman he always kept his eye on. Her name was Flavia Menses, and every day, she came into SPQB for a hot burdock water and a sun-warmed raisin bagel with fermented anchovy paste.

This woman is fantastic! She comes into the store and I just melt like a piece of poorly made beeswax. I glance over her gluteus maximus, her vastus lateralis, and her supraspinatus, and I thank the household gods that major muscle groups are identified by their Latin names. Today, I finally had the cohonem to reveal my

attraction to her; O sorry man I am! I am so inept at this sort of thing. I had just handed over her usual bagel and burdock water and muttered something about what a beautiful day it is (I am as tongue-tied as a slave being tortured by Draco whenever I see Flavia!). She smiled and I decided to be bold. I told her how much I love when she comes into the store and I asked her if she would go to the Colosseum with me some day to watch the gladiators. Stupid idea, of course; women hate the Colosseum. Why, oh why, didn't I suggest the mvsevm? Anyway, she responded, "Oh, Sol. You and I can never be together, for you are a Jew and I am a, er, um, a Roman!" I felt there was something she wasn't telling me. What could it be? No matter what, I knew I loved her. Nothing she could say would ever change my mind about that. She probably wasn't Jewish, but who cares? I believe that someday I will live to see a new era of love between all peoples (except the slaves, of course. Let's not get carried away here).

—Journal of Sol Yutstein,
dated IV Nones of Janus, Nero X

Although he believed in tolerance, free love, and representative democracy, Yutstein considered himself a loyal Roman and, as such, enjoyed going to the Colosseum to see the Christians get thrown to the lions. You could bring a few sandwiches and watch for hours. Plus, the Colosseum was a great place to see a mauling. As the Roman historian Martial tells us, even from the cheap seats you could hear the sound of the lion's teeth against the victim's bones. (It is widely known that the design for Baltimore's popular Camden Yards

Stadium mimicked the Colosseum's sight lines.) One day, Yutstein was sitting in the upper deck when he was shocked to see Flavia Menses be thrown into the ring, accused by Emperor Nero of being one of the Christians who set the city aflame earlier in the year. "Flavia?! Flavia?! A Christian? Who knew?" Yutstein was no hero, but he knew he had to do something to save the woman he loved. To hear him tell it, he jumped down from the upper deck, ran through the box seats to the field, and soon found himself in the ring with Flavia.

Sol Yutstein's Heroic Rescue: Was It Possible?

Archeologists who study crowd flow in ancient coliseums dispute Sol Yutstein's version of his heroic rescue of Flavia Menses from the lions at the Colosseum in Rome. Measurements of the stadium's dimensions from ancient blueprints show that the upper deck at the Colosseum did not have sufficient overhang to allow Yutstein to jump from one deck to the other in the manner he described.[*] It was far more likely that he simply took the stairs. Yes, history is clear that he did save Flavia Menses's life that day, but the latest research has cast doubt on the accuracy of Yutstein's journal.

[*] Rosencranz, Jakob, *Upper Tier Architecture in Ancient Roman Arena Design, 24 BC–AD 116.* Obscure University Press, 1987.

"I can't believe you never told me!" Yutstein said. "I love you, Flavia." Flavia had more immediate concerns on her mind. "That's great, Sol, but can we talk about it after we get out of here?" By this time, the lion had been released into the ring and was slowly circling the happy couple. "Get out of here?" Yutstein said. "Who do I look like? Septimus Maximus? That lion is going to chew me up like a fresh bialy."

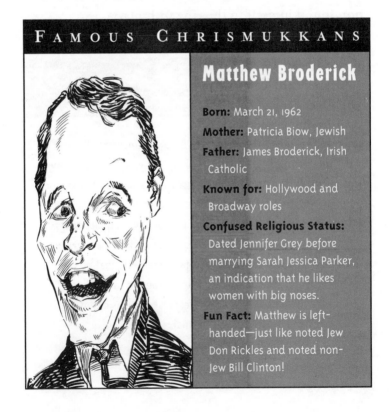

FAMOUS CHRISMUKKANS

Matthew Broderick

Born: March 21, 1962

Mother: Patricia Biow, Jewish

Father: James Broderick, Irish Catholic

Known for: Hollywood and Broadway roles

Confused Religious Status: Dated Jennifer Grey before marrying Sarah Jessica Parker, an indication that he likes women with big noses.

Fun Fact: Matthew is left-handed—just like noted Jew Don Rickles and noted non-Jew Bill Clinton!

But suddenly, Yutstein had an idea. "A bialy! Yes, that's it, of course!" He opened his satchel and threw a dozen bialys at the lion, who had great difficulty masticating them (history tells us they were day-olds). Yutstein grabbed Flavia's hand and the couple rushed to the exit—but the Emperor's elite guards moved to intercept them. Yutstein's journal recounts what happened next:

I prayed to Jupiter—the god, not the planet—and then even beseeched Poseidon, until I realized that we Romans call him Neptune, and that he wouldn't really be that useful in this particular crisis anyway. But I swore, by Mars!, that I would never be taken alive. Fortunately, I knew the centurions. They were regular customers at SPQB! Alas, I regretted my decision to never give them a discount. What was I thinking? You should always give cops and firefighters a discount! As Ceres is my witness, it will never happen again. Anyway, as the centurions moved in, I quickly promised them a bottomless cup of hot Egyptian blackwater and a fresh bagel or bialy at SPQB or even at Bagelus Maximus, my downtown store, every day for a year if they'd let me and Flavia go. After a brief negotiation—two praetors held out for bagels with schmear—we were allowed to leave.

—Journal of Sol Yutstein,
dated IX Ides of September, Nero X

At first, their lives were a struggle of cultural clashes, both journals indicate. Flavia insisted, for example, on closing the bagel store on Sundays, while Yutstein

What Was in Flavia Menses's Night-Table Drawer?

Historians were, of course, fascinated by the discovery of Sol Yutstein and Flavia Menses's journals, but archeologists were drawn to Flavia's bedside table, which had been unearthed in the same dig. In the drawer was a long cylindrical piece of smoothly polished marble with the words "Supremus Maximus" carved into the side. I subsequently wrote about the discovery of both the piece of marble and Flavia's diary in the *Journal of the Ancient Chrismukkan*, the leading scholarly publication catering to those of us who study Chrismukkah traditions between the birth of Christ and the seventh century. Unfortunately, it was the vaguely phallic piece of marble that became a lightning rod for controversy. Professor Richard Broadhurst at Harvard argued in his paper, "The Centurion in the Night-Table Drawer: Flavia Menses, Sol Yutstein, and the Challenge of Pre-Renaissance Sexual Satisfaction," that its discovery was evidence that the Yutstein-Menses marriage was so deeply flawed that Menses was reduced to gratifying herself with a common sexual aid modeled on the genitals of a popular gladiator of the day. But Professor Philip Morgenjohansenberg-enspiegel of the University of Copenhagen rebutted Broadhurst in his paper, "Girls Just Wanna Have Fun: The Danger of Judging the First-Century Flavia Menses with a Twenty-First-Century Morality System." Morgenjohansenbergenspiegel suggested that the device merely spiced up the Yutstein-Menses marriage and should not be interpreted as evidence that Yutstein was failing to live up to his Talmudic responsibility to satisfy his wife. The Jewish Yutstein, after all, was a virgin when he married, while the Christian Menses was so sexually experienced that she was widely known throughout ancient Rome—not just the city, mind you, but the entire empire, from southern Gaul to Sumeria—as "the woman who put the 'ho' in 'Holy Roman Empire.'" He couldn't hold out any hope of satisfying Flavia, at least in those early days. My subsequent scholarship would reveal that Yutstein later became quite an accomplished lover, thanks to his discovery of the aphrodisiac qualities of rhinoceros horn, but the publication of my paper was repeatedly delayed until it became moot anyway: Broadhurst bludgeoned Morgenjohan-senbergenspiegel to death at a scholarly conference.

preferred Saturdays. And when Yutstein invented the world's first bagel sandwiches, Flavia demanded that the store offer shrimp salad. And when Yutstein was toying with the idea of bagel chips, Flavia briefly tried marketing them as "Body-of-Christ crisps."

But Sol and Flavia were devoted to each other. Unable to agree on whether to celebrate the Jewish New Year in September or the Christian version on January 1, Sol and Flavia celebrated New Year's Eve on May 19. On Sundays, Sol refused to drink the blood of Christ, but he did agree to consume an entire bottle of red wine. For her part, Flavia refused to wrap her arms in the sacred phylacteries at the synagogue on Saturday mornings, but she had no objection to being tied up on Saturday nights. And, eventually, they had two children, whom they raised with a mixture of Jewish and Christian traditions. They did coin the term "Chrismukkah," but neither side of their families was in any rush to join them.

FAMOUS CHRISMUKKANS

John Houseman

1902–1988

Mother: English

Father: French-born Jew

Known for: Pompous acting style

Confused Religious Status: Was Jewish, yet used his acting to champion the old money/anti-Semitic pretensions of a variety of stodgy institutions.

Fun Fact: John's birth name was actually Jacques Haussmann!

That much is clear from Flavia's journal. "It is so unfair!" she wrote in an entry dated 14 Avgvst, Nero XI. "My sister, Heroditia, refuses to even meet Sol, the man who saved my life in the Colosseum. The other day, I invited her to our wedding, and she said, 'I won't come to your wedding, but I will dance at your funeral!' And then she ripped her tunic and said I was dead to her."

Two days later, there's a similar entry: "After my sister's reaction, I thought I'd seen everything, but Sol's family is no better. When I invited them to our Chrismukkah dinner, his mother said she couldn't make it because she wanted to go to the Temple of Apollo to watch the season premiere of *That '70s BCE Show*. I thought that was so cold."

With their families abandoning them, Sol and Flavia created their own holiday traditions every Chrismukkah. It started with a simple ritual—the chewing of day-old bialys but before long included many of the Chrismukkah rituals celebrated all over the world today. From the consumption of salty fried potatoes to the Hour of Silent Reflection to the refusing of the gifts, many of Chrismukkah's greatest traditions—described in full in Chapter 3—can trace their origins to the groundbreaking marriage of Sol Yutstein and Flavia Menses.

CHAPTER 2

How Modern Chrismukkah Was Born

I have seen the volumes on the library shelves
And an old man on Main Street with a pair of elves
Saying "Do you have your Chrismukkah herbs?"
I haven't seen the like outside the cities and burbs
Oh, daddy, is this really where it starts?
To be at Chrismukkah without the Queen of Hearts
        —Bob Dylan, *"Stuck with Ruby and Josephine*
                    at the Chrismukkah Party"

DRISCOLL WAS ON THE PHONE AGAIN, back at the dig in Bethlehem.

"Kuntzman, I have some bad news for you," he said. I expected the worst: that the Gospel of Zebulon and the Book of Rotations he'd found in that Bethlehem landfill were fakes. Everyone knew that I'd been burned before by counterfeit antiquities, and when I heard the anxious tone in Driscoll's voice, all my past controversies hit me in the gut: the Genghis Khan diaries, the Pope Innocent VI sex tapes, the *Eva Braun Bunker Cookbook*. I'd fallen prey to historic forgeries a few times before, and my reputation would certainly not survive another such disaster. Fortunately, the news was not so bad.

"The Gospel of Zebulon and the Book of Rotations that I discovered are copies!" Driscoll said. For a top archeologist, uncovering copies instead of originals is like a Hollywood casting agent bedding a young starlet only to find that her breasts are real.

"Copies? How can you be sure?"

"After you left, I did a microscopic analysis of the papyrus and found a tiny notation in the corner of every page: It said, '2/10.' That means that I was looking at only one of ten copies of the document. Oh, and there was a receipt at the bottom of the urn from Kinkstein's Scribery for 10 shekels. That was probably the biggest giveaway."

I had a much bigger concern, of course, and Driscoll anticipated my thoughts.

"Not to worry, pal," he said. "The scrolls may be copies, but the text is real. They're direct replicas of the Gospel of Zebulon and the Book of Rotations."

"So you mean—," I said, but was interrupted.

"Yes, you can continue your analysis of them. This is not going to be another controversy, like that time you claimed to have found Shakespeare's long-lost play, *Battlestar Andromeda*."

"Look, I just want you to know that—"

"I know. I have your full support. I appreciate that."

"No, what I was trying to say is that I—"

"I know. Of course, I will keep searching for the original books. They're probably still there in the same garbage dump. I can't wait to sink my teeth into that rotting filth! But hey, that's who I am. I'm an archeologist!"

"No, what I was trying to say—if you'd just shut up—is that I have to go move the car so I don't get a ticket," I finally said. But I didn't merely move the car from one side of the street to the other; I headed straight to JFK to catch the first flight to Byelorussia. Four hours later—don't blame me, blame the Long Island Expressway—I was at the ticket counter.

"I need a coach ticket to Minsk, please," I told the Aeroflot agent. "One way. This could take a while."

Knowledge, Truth, and Bitterness: The Minsk Conclave of 1342

Once we reached cruising altitude, I refreshed my memory about the illustrious history of Minsk, which in the 1300s was the center of Jewish intellectual thought. Sure, the city hasn't been much since the largest employer, an apparel manufacturer called Minsk Minks, went belly up. But in medieval times, Minsk was home to six universities, a dozen scholarly institutes, at least fifteen libraries, and forty opticians. There had once been just one university, run by the Grand Rabbi, Menachem Goldstein, but he quarreled with his second in command, the Slightly Less Grand Rabbi, Shmuel Molberg, who broke from his mentor and formed his own center of learning, Anti-Goldstein University (motto: "Holding a Grudge Since 1312"). Of course, it wasn't more than a few years before Molberg's best student, Akiva Rosenblatt, broke from his mentor and formed his own school, Counter-Molberg College of Anti-Goldstein Study ("Knowledge, Truth, and Bitterness"). Rosenblatt was later betrayed by a group of his own students, who formed their own school, The New School for Anti-Rosenblatt, Pro-Molberg, Goldstein-Neutral Study ("Independence in the Pursuit of Acrimony"). And similar schisms occurred at all the remaining colleges. As a result, the Great Thinkers of

Minsk were universally acknowledged to be the greatest minds of the world yet could not agree on anything
at all. If Molberg passed Goldstein in the street, even a
benign conversation about the weather could provoke
the bitterest of tirades.

"Hello, Rabbi," Molberg once said to Goldstein.
"Isn't it a lovely day?"

"I shall not be baited by you, Molberg! I refuse to
answer until I understand your definition of 'lovely.'"

"By 'lovely,' I mean simply that it is temperate with
very little humidity."

"Ah, ha! Another trap! I happen to appreciate
some humidity, as it allows my side curls to retain their
shape."

And that was relatively polite, by Minsk standards.
Once, a harmless exchange between Goldstein and
Rosenblatt about the pitching staff of the Minsk Dreidls
ended in such vituperation that Rosenblatt's students
burned Goldstein's college to the ground. Years later,
the High Court ruled that Rosenblatt's students had
acted appropriately: Goldstein was, indeed, wrong about
the strength of the Dreidls' bullpen.

The director of Counter-Molberg College of Anti-
Goldstein Study had been trying for years to get me
to Minsk to study a set of what he claimed were
authentic biblical scrolls. I dismissed him out of hand—
probably the reaction I should've had when that Ukrainian arms dealer told me he could get me a cache of

Lenin's love letters to Karl Marx for next to nothing—but once Driscoll gave me the news about the Bethlehem copies, I recalled his invitation.

When I got to Minsk, I headed straight for the college. The scrolls were waiting for me. Driscoll had told me what to look for, and, sure enough, there was no notation to indicate that these were copies. There were some beet stains on them, but I attributed that to the fact that the Gospel of Zebulon and the Book of Rotations were so hard to put down that the medieval scholars would often eat their dinner right there at the library table.

And even more important than the scrolls, the college also owned an invaluable artifact: a transcript of the world's only known rabbinical conference on their meaning. Because of the importance of the text, all of the ideological parties of Minsk had made an unprecedented vow to work together to try to decode their mysteries. But the détente only lasted for a few days. Rosenblatt believed that the Gospel of Zebulon was a parable which revealed that the Messiah would return that very year on the twenty-third day of the month of Sislev in the town of Vinsk-Bretofsk—and he started accepting "donations" so he could make the trip. He was later repudiated when it turned out that he was having an affair with a Vinsk-Bretofsk woman. Molberg was convinced that the very same passage contained all the rules for living a pious life, including a complete abstinence from pork, shellfish, and that sticky egg salad sold in diners. Goldstein read the gospel as a mathematical equation that, when all the letters were converted into their numerical equivalents, had nothing at all to do with the sacrament but did offer a fantastic recipe for roast chicken. The conference was over before it even started.

FAMOUS CHRISMUKKANS

Fritz Lang

1890–1976

Mother: Paula Schlesinger, born Jewish, but converted to Catholicism

Father: Anton Lang, devoutly Catholic

Known for: Groundbreaking, experimental films

Confused Religious Status: He was Catholic but turned down the Nazis, who wanted him to make propaganda films.

Fun Fact: Fritz left Germany, but his Nazi-sympathizing wife stayed behind—so he divorced her!

But thanks to a request from the mayor of Minsk, the warring parties agreed to hold a second conference to come to some consensus. It also didn't go well. At the opening reception, the mayor greeted the participants and invited them to enjoy the refreshments that his staff had laid out. Goldstein took exception to the honey cake, seeing it as a clear repudiation of his recent paper, "Mind Your Own Beeswax: Natural and Artificial Sweeteners in the Five Books of Moses." Molberg was offended that no one had removed the crusts from the finger sandwiches. "As Abraham circumcised Isaac, so must these sandwiches be consecrated before the Lord." Even Rosenblatt, who enjoyed a buffet like no other scholar, was troubled by the lack of any beef dish. "There's nothing troublesome from a biblical perspective, of course," he said. "I just happen to like beef. Especially a brisket." All of the scholars threatened to walk out until the mayor appealed to their vanity by reminding them that they constituted the greatest collection of minds in the entire world. All of the scholars nodded knowingly, warmed by the mayor's compliment—but each told himself that he was the greatest of the great minds.

According to the transcript, the first official conclave was held on June 13, 1342, in a private room of Moishe's Rabbinical College and Knishery, a neutral setting. All of the top thinkers of Minsk were in attendance, including Goldstein; Molberg; Rosenblatt; Menachem Bindler, who once definitively proved that God has six faces and that, coincidentally, they were all his; Aleksandr Roskolnik, who argued that the kosher rules had been misinterpreted for centuries and that God wanted his Chosen People to eat pork—but the Lord permitted only pigs raised on Roskolnik's brother-in-law's organic farm outside Pinsk; and, of course, the elderly scholar Benyamin Solokovnetz, who was not known for any specific discovery or interpretation, but whose wife was the cleaning lady at the knishery and tended to wear low-cut dresses when vacuuming. The transcript can still teach us lessons today about the role of the intellectual in society, the importance of honest debate, and the need for security guards at scholarly conferences:

GOLDSTEIN: Let us get to work, my fellow scholars.

MOLBERG: I am fascinated with Rotations' view of the shepherds. As you know, this is the only place in the Bible where shepherds are so repudiated. Rotations even uses the phrase "smelly, uncivilized, loathsome brutes."

BINDLER: Perhaps Rotations wants us to reconsider the shepherd. After all, did not the Wise Men, having spent several days in the malodorous presence of shepherds, decide to not only share their sacred crop with them, but actually agree to meet them every year at the same spot for more rejoicing?

ROSKOLNIK: Bindler, you idiot! Zebulon also points out that the Wise Men failed to return each year, as promised! Is there anything more pathetic than the spectacle of the stinking shepherds returning to the empty campsite to wait for the Wise Men? It's like one of those pointless existential comedies!

MOLBERG: I should also point out that they fasted between meals. I believe this is a valuable lesson. We should refrain from snacking.

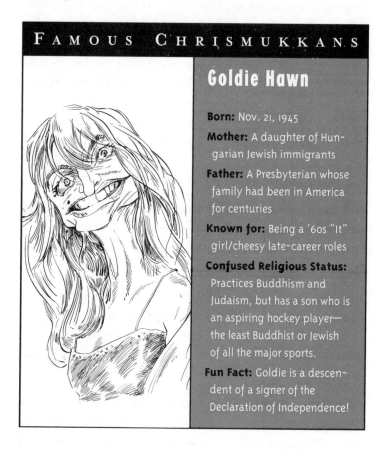

FAMOUS CHRISMUKKANS

Goldie Hawn

Born: Nov. 21, 1945

Mother: A daughter of Hungarian Jewish immigrants

Father: A Presbyterian whose family had been in America for centuries

Known for: Being a '60s "It" girl/cheesy late-career roles

Confused Religious Status: Practices Buddhism and Judaism, but has a son who is an aspiring hockey player—the least Buddhist or Jewish of all the major sports.

Fun Fact: Goldie is a descendent of a signer of the Declaration of Independence!

BINDLER: Surely a carrot or green pepper dipped in hummus is acceptable?

MOLBERG: Oh, sure, it's acceptable—if you want to spend all eternity up to your kishkas in the flaming oil of Hell! No snacks! Never.

ROSKOLNIK: It is exactly that kind of inflexibility that makes you a great scholar, Molberg, but a lousy lover.

GOLDSTEIN: Friends, I remain fascinated by the herb in the dried-out sheep stomach. First of all, what herb was it?

ROSENBLATT: Clearly, it is hallucinogenic mushrooms! I happen to know that they were widely cultivated on the eastern slope of the Dead Sea around the time of the stable birth of the False Messiah.

BINDLER: You must be on hallucinogenic mushrooms, Rosenblatt! Zebulon clearly describes the herb as being green and leafy. Clearly, marijuana.

ROSKOLNIK: Broccoli rabe!

ALL: Broccoli rabe?!

ROSKOLNIK: Recall, brothers, how Rotations refers to the Fourth Gift as having a thick stem and leaves? While it is known that Herod the Great inhaled the burned smoke of merely the leaves, we know from Rotations that others would eat the entire stalk, from stem to leaves. Clearly, broccoli rabe.

BINDLER: This is absurdity! If we are to go solely on your interpretation, Roskolnik, why is it not leeks? Or scallions? Or asparagus? Or even that broccoli-asparagus hybrid I tried last week at Judea's—broccolini, I think he called it. Clearly, the Lord is trying to give us the Biblical cover to legalize marijuana—and yet you persist that the Almighty merely wanted us to eat more broccoli?! (To the others) Am I missing something, or is he an idiot?

ROSENBLATT: Oh, he's an idiot all right. Rotations tells us that the shepherds returned to the encampment every year without fail. Who does that for broccoli rabe?

BINDLER: But they did eventually give up, did they not, Roskolnik? Does not Rotations tell us that the shepherds disbanded to all corners of the globe?

SOLOKOVNETZ: Watch that "globe" talk, Bindler. I still have whip marks from the last time I said the world was round. But I understand your point. I believe that in the shepherd's diaspora, we have the essential purpose of this holiday: Whereas most celebratory gatherings involve the coming together of families, I believe the scrolls are telling us to create a holiday that would allow us to commemorate the gathering of the Wise Men and the shepherds as far away from our families as possible.

GOLDSTEIN: Solokovnetz, you have done it again! I know we've quarreled over your belief that Moses should have extinguished the Burning Bush—he was the fire control officer in his building, after all—but this interpretation is your best ever.

MOLBERG: I am forced to agree. What I wouldn't give for a holiday where I didn't have to eat my sister-in-law's tzimmes! I got a restraining order, so she switched to flanken—but then I got the gout!

GOLDSTEIN: So we are agreed, then: The head of the household will be given an hour-long break shortly after the arrival of his wife's family.

MOLBERG: I believe we shall call this the "Hour of Silent Reflection."

SOLOKOVNETZ: Yes, that is very good. But I would argue that the Hour of Silent Reflection should re-create, as best as possible, the moment when the Wise Men shared their herb with the shepherds.

ROSENBLATT: He's good, this kid.

MOLBERG: We'll need other rituals, too. Perhaps the story of Solomon and Leah can provide an example for us: Our holiday symbol should be salted potatoes—the saltier, the better!

SOLOKOVNETZ: Can we leave the salt to personal taste? My doctor says I need to cut back. And perhaps there are other dishes from Solomon's Eastern tradition and Leah's Jewish roots that we could merge into a unifying cuisine?

GOLDSTEIN: As long as you don't call it "fusion." My wife took me to that new Thai-Ukrainian place on Federovna Prospekt last night. Who puts cilantro in borscht?! But Solokovnetz is right. We should have one day a year when we can toss aside the kosher rules. Have you ever had the Pork Loin with Creamed Oyster Stuffing at Pius's

Place next to the church on Divinity Street? I know it's a sin—sinfully delicious, that is!

MOLBERG: I am also quite fascinated by the Christian practice of gift-giving. I find it excessive, don't you? I mean, they are supposed to be commemorating the birth of their supposed messiah—the one we supposedly killed—yet all they do is spend money on useless gifts. It is a clear misunderstanding of Zebulon, which states clearly that the shepherds *refused* the three gifts that the Wise Men later placed at the feet of the baby Jesus.

SOLOKOVNETZ: Are you accusing the Wise Men of regifting?

MOLBERG: It's right there in the Scripture! The shepherd Ezekiel turned down the very gifts that later became symbols of Christian materialistic excess!

GOLDSTEIN: Let us rejoice, then, brothers, that we have found a path away from that wantonness! A strict interpretation of Zebulon makes it clear that family members and friends should offer a variety of gifts, all of which should be politely refused.

ROSENBLATT: At this point, I think the only thing we've forgotten is a song. Every good holiday has a song that sort of captures the spirit of the event. You know, Passover has "Dayenu," Rosh Hashanah has "Tapuchim Udvash." Even Hanukkah has that annoying dreidl song. Given what we know about the Wise Men and the shepherds, I believe that song should be called "Fellas, Let's Wait Some More." I've taken the liberty of writing out some lyrics:

Fellas, Let's Wait Some More

Words and Music by Akiva Rosenblatt

They said they'd be back here this year
But again they've left us alone.
It's not that I'm filled up with fear
But I wish we had more than this shriveled lamb bone

Yes, we shared but four days of joy
It was brief, but the time was superb
To be with such wizened old boys
To sing, to dance, and partake of their wondrous herb!

Chorus:
So fellas, let's wait some more
They asked us to return and we swore
So fellas, put away those moans
And we'll soon satisfy our jones
So if they never give us their bonus
I won't start to disbelieve
Those Wise Men may have disowned us
So pass me that pipe, those matches, and some leaves

After that meeting of the great minds, Chrismukkah, once celebrated by isolated families who did not even know that other people were marking the same holiday, became a fairly common celebration.

America's First Chrismukkans

Upon my return from Minsk, I found myself obsessed with discovering how Chrismukkah made it to America, where it is as popular as any holiday, with the possible exception of Arbor Day. I'd barely unpacked my bags, but clearly, it was time for more travel. My destination: the Museum of the American Pilgrim in Plymouth, Massachusetts. Unfortunately, my minuscule grant from the National Endowment for the Understanding of Tangential Eastern Religions (NEUTER) was practically exhausted, so I hopped a Fung Wah bus out of Chinatown to Boston. I marveled at the $15 ticket price and was pleased that there are still some proud companies willing to sacrifice such things as motor vehicle inspections, routine maintenance, and thickness of tire tread to keep costs down.

At the museum, I reviewed the passenger manifest of the *Mayflower* and found that there were 154 Christians, 22 Jews, and 15 slaves on board. And then, written below the list of names in the elaborate cursive of the era, was this simple entry: "Other: four." Other? What could "other" mean? If slaves were given their own line in the manifest, "other" must have certainly been a group of people considered subhuman by the mores of the time.

In the museum library, I read up on the first Thanksgiving celebration between the Pilgrims and the Native

Americans, whose generous assistance to the hungry, bedraggled newcomers would later be paid back with massacres and expulsion. That story is widely known, but very little has been written about the first Christmas and Hanukkah celebrated by the Pilgrims a month later. Thanks to my unfettered access to the museum's collection, I was able to review the original diaries of

Early Chrismukkah Celebrations Around the World

After the famous Minsk Conclave of 1342, which laid down many of the basic rituals for Chrismukkah, the holiday really took off. But there were many local variations on the traditions. Early Norwegian adherents, for example, would find the tallest blond student in the town and festoon him with wax figurines of the miraculous dried-out sheep stomach. Romanian peasants would sacrifice a tax accountant. French tradesmen would empty three fine casks and race drunkenly through the town atop them. And Welsh farmers would take the intestines of their sickliest goat, fill them with inedible gristle, cook them, and leave them at the steps of the Roman Catholic monastery for unsuspecting vagrants. But thanks to an almost complete lack of communication between nations during the so-called Dark Ages, no one knew how Chrismukkah was being celebrated by other cultures.

FAMOUS CHRISMUKKANS

Harrison Ford

Born: July 13, 1942

Mother: Dora Nidelman, Jewish

Father: Christopher Ford, Irish/German Catholic

Known for: High-grossing films/demands for privacy

Confused Religious Status: Asked what religion he practices, he once said "Democrat."

Fun Fact: Harrison worked as a carpenter (just like Jesus) after initial failure as an actor (quite unlike Jesus)!

William Bradford, the leader of the Plymouth colony, who was extremely dismissive of the four residents who celebrated neither holiday:

In the name of Lorde God, Amen. I would not wish to have them populated among us in the Colonie, but they are here and, mostly, performing their jobs. When I invited them to the towne square to partake of the Christmas feast and to celebrate the Birth of the

Christ childe, they refused. When the Jewish rabbi bade them to mark the Hanukkah miracle, they also refused. I started watching them more closely and noticed that they differ from us in many Wayes. They have angered many of the colonists by refusing to add the letter *e* to many common Nounes; they believe it superfluous. As a test, I presented them with a small Gifte, and they promptly refused it. I do not understand their Strange manners. They are not technically in violation of the Mayflower Compacte, but they bother Me.

Bradford may not have understood, but I did: Chrismukkans! Historians had always known that four Chrismukkans were burned at the stake after the Salem witch trials, but it has always been believed that those Chrismukkans had started celebrating the holiday once they arrived in the New World. I had discovered that they brought the holiday with them. While this might not seem like a particularly huge distinction, it did earn me another $10,000 from NEUTER, which I used to buy a Mini Cooper, which I then promptly drove to Salem to review the transcripts of the famous Chrismukkan trial of 1699. Unlike the witches, who were executed for sorcery, the Chrismukkans—Shmuel and Betsy Smythe-Glickstein and Anthony and Manya Polishek-D'Angelo— were facing condemnation at the stake for the crime of Nonconformitie, according to the prosecution report.

If this Colonie is to survive, we must all Believe in the same things. Yet these poor Souls seem not to care for the Conventions and

Traditions of the Colonie. They do not accept Giftes, they do not Pray, they remove themselves for an Hour, they consume stale Bread and make Burnt Offerings for inhaling. Their Potato dishes are very heavie on the Salt, too.

The Salem prosecutors could not have known it at the time, of course, but by killing the four Chrismukkans, they were only creating martyrs. True, Chrismukkah was temporarily wiped out of the New World, but references to the Chrismukkan struggle continued to pop up throughout American history. When Lewis and Clark spotted the Pacific in December 1805, for example, the pair celebrated by frying potatoes, with Clark writing in his journal, "Ocian [sic] in view! O! The joy! Meriwether has started frying potatoes and I am in search of a small gift to give him, nothing extravagant, as I know he will return it to me promptly." In the midst of the Civil War, Abraham Lincoln wrote in his journal, "O great Providence, it is Christmastime again, but I am writing with a heavy Hearte for now we are engaged in a great War. As I pause to celebrate the birth of Your only Sonne, the Miracle of Judah Maccabee's victory over the Tyrant Antiochus, and the union of Leah and Solomon, my only hope is that Democracy can survive and that all of Your children will celebrate Christmas, Hanukkah, and Chrismukkah in Peace and Prosperitie." And in the 1950s, members of an atheistic commune outside of Portland, Oregon, set out across the country in a

tangerine-colored Volkswagen bus to spread the story of
St. Shmuel, St. Betsy, St. Anthony, and St. Manya.

The Chrismukkah
Rights Movement

Naturally, the holiday was sneered at by the "estab-
lishment," which had a vested interest in maintain-
ing the popularity and, therefore, economic viability
of the existing holidays. In a polemic published by the
American Celebrant in 1925, noted social critic E. B. White
wrote, "I don't understand the 'Chrismukkah' holiday.
Are there not enough completely satisfactory celebratory
days with which we can occasion our faith?" That same
year, fiery orator Roscoe Tanner wrote in *Gunton's Maga-
zine*, "The entire exercise of Chrismukkah strikes me as
skindullkeragally," although it has been lost to history
which meaning of the word "skindullkeragally" he was
using. And in 1928, when the promoters of Chrismukkah were in full flight from mainstream society, editori-
alist Cranston Johns with the *Mississippi Klansman* gloated,
"Cast thee away, O Chrismukkans, into the dark recesses
of thy soul-less despair! Thou deservest only death—and
not a clean death, either, but a very horrible, painful
death." Johns's views were hardly extreme—he went on
to serve six terms in the House, after all—but he was
forced to resign when it was discovered that he had long

been having an affair with his Chrismukkan secretary, who did not even know how to type.

Still, the anti-Chrismukkah sentiment ran so strongly in this country that at various times during the 1930s and 1940s, twenty-four states banned Chrismukkah outright, while another ten forbade all "faith-neutral, gift-free celebrations of more than two people." Even though the Nevada Supreme Court—in the landmark 1945 case, Schimmelberger-Thomas v. Nevada—threw out explicit Chrismukkah bans, vague anti-Chrismukkah language remained on the books in most states for decades. Many states eventually legalized Chrismukkah, but strictly forbade what had become a holiday tradition—the consumption of "broccoli rabe"—although it was occasionally tolerated by local police forces. Only after sheriff's deputies raided a Chrismukkah celebration outside of Ann Arbor in 1982, arresting forty-two Chrismukkans and confiscating sixty kilos of a particularly pungent variety of Panamanian broccoli rabe did the United States Supreme Court agree to hear the case. In the case—Harris-Schnitzelgruber v. Meese—the Chrismukkah followers argued that the Washtenaw County sheriffs had no right under the First, Fourth, Sixth, and Twenty-First Amendments to disrupt a private religious function, regardless of whether it included the consumption of Panamanian broccoli rabe, which had become a controlled substance under President Reagan. Oral arguments were contentious. Chrismukkan lead counsel Alan Dershowitz offered a classic argument in

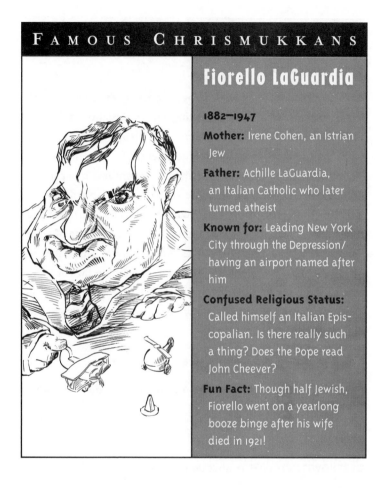

Fiorello LaGuardia

1882–1947

Mother: Irene Cohen, an Istrian Jew

Father: Achille LaGuardia, an Italian Catholic who later turned atheist

Known for: Leading New York City through the Depression/ having an airport named after him

Confused Religious Status: Called himself an Italian Episcopalian. Is there really such a thing? Does the Pope read John Cheever?

Fun Fact: Though half Jewish, Fiorello went on a yearlong booze binge after his wife died in 1921!

favor of the separation of church and state, but as the transcript shows, Chief Justice William Rehnquist tried to keep the debate simply to the facts in the case:

REHNQUIST: Mr. Dershowitz, are your clients not, in fact, asking this Court to sign off on legalizing the consumption of hallucinogenic vegetables?

DERSHOWITZ: Mr. Chief Justice, they are asking the Court for nothing of the sort. What they are asking for, in actuality, is the right to be left alone. Alone, your honor, to celebrate their faith beyond the prying eyes and moral judgments of a government that has no compelling interest in whether they consume broccoli rabe or whether they stick to the more socially acceptable deep-fried latkes or butter-rich fruitcake. I will remind this court that such traditional holiday fare is laden with fat, a known cause of childhood obesity and Type II diabetes. Could we not argue that the government has a compelling interest in preventing the consumption of these socially detrimental foodstuffs? Of course not. This very Court would wisely reject any government effort to ban such holiday foodstuffs.

REHNQUIST: Mr. Dershowitz, you are out of order!

DERSHOWITZ: *I'm* out of order? *You're* out of order! This whole *proceeding* is out of order!

REHNQUIST: Oh, is that the truth?

DERSHOWITZ: Truth?! Truth?! Do you want the truth?!

REHNQUIST: Actually, I can't handle the truth! Please sit down!

Despite the exchange, Rehnquist failed to carry the day. Writing for the 7-2 majority, Justice Thurgood Marshall fully accepted Dershowitz's argument. "One could argue that the U.S. government should prevent holiday celebrants from doing damage to their bodies that could later cause them to overwhelm the health care system. But this government does not have—and, indeed, this Court would not grant—the right to pick and choose which holiday traditions it will allow and which it will forbid. Therefore, I say to you, let them eat greasy potato pancakes! Let them eat fatty fruitcake! Let them burn broccoli rabe!" *Harris-Schnitzelgruber v. Meese*, 324 U.S. 44 (1982).

Marshall's ruling has widely been credited with causing the great surge in Chrismukkah celebrations that continues today.

CHAPTER 3

The Rituals of Chrismukkah

I like Chrismukkah,
I like it all year long.
A day with no gifts or Gods,
From Newark to Hong Kong.

—Dorothy Parker, *"Letter from an*
Unrepentant Chrismukkan," 1935

JUST AS JEWS MARK the Passover holiday by retelling the story of their exodus from slavery in Egypt, and Christians recount the birth of Jesus at Midnight Mass every year, Chrismukkans have their own set rituals when observing the holiday. Most of the common traditions were established at the Minsk Convention, but still others have developed over the years.

The Reading of the Four Short, Easy-to-Remember Directives

Chrismukkans were once like other holiday celebrants, devoting hours telling and retelling their sacred stories. Jews, for example, are saddled at Passover with a seemingly endless reading of a Haggadah, which not only tells the story of the ancient Israelites' flight from bondage in Egypt, but also includes the megillah, a dense chapter that recounts the banal debate between medieval rabbis over the symbolic meaning of every sentence in the Torah. That's bad enough, but in some Orthodox branches of Judaism, the entire megillah must be recited while attempting to ascend a greased pole with a banana in one hand. Modern Christians are also burdened by a late-night Christmas Eve mass, much of which is recited in Latin and Gibberish. Yes, the Church does deserve some credit for keeping those ancient languages alive, but many Catholics, even religious ones, have complained of the difficulty of sitting through Midnight Mass knowing that they still have to assemble two kids' bicycles before dawn.

But thanks to the Chrismukkah Reformation of 1845—which occurred after several Chrismukkan families complained that they could no longer devote 36 hours to commemorating the holiday—Chrismukkah demands only a quick restatement of principles before moving on to the central rituals of the day. These principles have been boiled down to four short, declarative sentences that are plucked from the essential core of the Chrismukkah story:

(a) Be nice to people whom you're initially inclined to not like.
(b) Stop making such a big deal about unforeseen changes in plans.
(c) Try to share—but always leave a little for yourself too.
(d) Always have on hand something that can distract a lion.

Many families have their own traditions about how the directives are read. The Sanchez-Rothsteins of Dover, Delaware, print them up on cards that are left at every guest's seat. The Cohen-Marcoses of St. Louis ask the youngest literate child to recite the Directives while eating a piece of ham on a matzo cracker. And the Cicciolini-Turetzkys of Brooklyn, New York, take off their clothes, smear their bodies with bacon fat, and make love on a tarpaulin on which is depicted the Battle of Agincourt. This isn't technically a Chrismukkah tradition, mind you. It's just something they enjoy.

The Burning of the Greenery

While it is inarguable that the first Chrismukkans burned green vegetation for four days while awaiting the birth of the so-called messiah, the substance that is burned varies greatly by region of the world. In the American Southwest, a small agave cactus is typically set afire. In China, the ceremonial vegetation is green tea leaves. In Africa, branches from a baobab tree are ignited by a torch bearing a flame from the previous year's celebration. And in Detroit, two hundred people once set fire to every green car in a three-block radius of the Pontiac Silverdome after a controversial playoff loss to the New York Jets. Local authorities remain unsure if this was a Chrismukkah celebration or a response to a referee's decision to give the Jets a first down with the score tied and 1:54 to go in the game, even though the instant replay clearly showed that Chad Pennington's fourth-down pass to Wayne Chrebet was incomplete. Either way, lots of green things were burned.

The Hour of
Silent Reflection

A lso a result of the Chrismukkah Reformation of
1845, a quiet hour is given to the head of the household, usually timed to the arrival of his in-laws. Many
families have combined the Burning of the Greenery and
this hour-long respite—and not just during Chrismukkah. In fact, in many families the expression, "I'm gonna
go burn the broccoli rabe," has become a euphemism for
a wide variety of activities.

The Measuring of
the Children

D uring the four-day period between their arrival in
the hills east of Bethlehem and the birth of the baby
Jesus, the Wise Men were so bored that they measured
each other for diversion. This has come down through
the ages as a fun game for all the kids. Of course, government bureaucrats have tried to appropriate the ritual
from a sacred article of faith to a public health initiative,
asking parents to not merely measure their children's
height, but also their weight, head radius, shoe size,
typing speed, 100-meter-dash time, and average stool
length, and then report the resulting Massive Body Index

to a central Department of Health and Human Services database. While many Americans have resisted, the database did help scientists definitively show there is no link between childhood obesity and typing speed.

The Chrismukkah Meal

Nowhere in the Gospel of Zebulon or the Book of Rotations is there any discussion of the Chrismukkah meal. But the marriage of Sol Yutstein and Flavia Menses, as well as the relationship of Solomon and Leah, has provided ample traditions for the holiday feast. When the guests are seated, the only thing on the table is a platter of day-old bialys, which are distributed by the head of the household. Each guest is expected to chew on the stale bread for a period no shorter than six minutes—the amount of time classical historians say it would have taken Yutstein and Menses to make their way from the center of the Colosseum floor through the side gate, out past the reserved parking for Senators and then through the plebian parking area, to the back room of Senatus Populus Que Bagelus, where they hid from authorities.

Next, the wife is expected to bring out a large platter of salty fried potatoes, and someone at the table is expected to bite into one of the potatoes even after receiving the admonition, "Don't bite into those potatoes yet. They're way too hot inside!" The resulting burned mouth is typically inundated with cold red sangria, which is not a Chrismukkah tradition at all, but, man, cold red sangria can be really refreshing sometimes.

The Singing of the Monotone Song

Inspired by the success of "Happy Birthday," which can be enjoyed in groups even if every singer is off-key, Rabbi Shmuel Molberg wrote up a prototype Chrismukkah song called "It's Chrismukkah Time." It is meant to be droned rather than sung. The words, known to all Chrismukkans, are simple, yet profound: "It's Chrismukkah time/It's Chrismukkah time/Time to celebrate Chrismukkah/Because my friends/It's Chrismukkah time." Despite its omnipresence in the public psyche, "It's Chrismukkah Time" is not in the public domain. Every year, Molberg's descendents reap hundreds of thousands of dollars in royalties from the use of "It's Chrismukkah Time" in countless movies and TV shows, the most famous, of course, being *Miracle on 47th Street*. And who could forget the Chrismukkah scene from *It's a Not So Bad Life When You Think About It*? Thanks to endless reruns of this classic, though knock-off, sequel, Jimmy Stewart's rendition of "It's Chrismukkah Time" has sold more copies any other holiday single, except for "Jingle Bells."

The Refusal of the Gift

Gift-giving is a main feature of many holidays—Christmas, Hanukkah, Flag Day. But Chrismukkah's ancient story has always centered on the moment when the shepherd Ezekiel turns down the Wise Men's gift of gold, frankincense, and myrrh and asks the Wise Men to give him and his fellow shepherds something else, something that the Wise Men seemed to want to keep for themselves. Throughout the centuries, this historic moment has become a powerful antimaterialistic statement. After the Singing of the Monotone Song, the eldest person present at the celebration is expected to pull out a large, nicely wrapped package and deliver it to the youngest male child. The child, in turn, is expected to accept the gift, give it a small shake, and then, without ceremony, say to the eldest person, "Thank you, but I have no use for this gift." The package is then returned to the giver.

Many cultures have interpreted this moment differently. In Scandinavia, the giver is then expected to donate the still-wrapped gift to charity. In India, the gift is opened anyway, just so the intended recipient can see what he missed out on. And in Bozeman, Montana, the Gilroy-Goldwassers sell the gift on eBay.

The Brief Consideration of
Taking Up a Collection
for Charity

Typically, upon the completion of the Refusal of
the Gift, the gift giver is expected to nod his head
knowingly and ponder the deeper meaning of the
refusal. Then, the giver is expected to recite from memory chapter 5, verses 42–48 from the Book of Rotations:
"Perhaps this is a good time to reconsider the materialism of our age, my friends. Perhaps we should redouble
our efforts to stop spending so much money on ourselves and devote ourselves to the well-being of others.
Perhaps we should return this gift and use the money to
build low-cost housing for a poor family in that slum
by the Jordan River. What do you say, my brothers?"
There is expected to be a pause, much nodding around
the table, and then the Brief Consideration of Taking Up a Collection for Charity. But the moment is
expected to pass when the head of the household delivers
the sacred words, "Anyone want seconds? More oyster
hamantaschen or gefilte shrimp? Any takers?"

The Half-Hearted Promise
to Start One's Diet
the Next Day

Although virtually all large family gatherings in virtually every culture end with vague grumbling about going on a diet, only Chrismukkah explicitly honors this tradition. The leader of the Chrismukkah festivities is expected to bemoan the gross excess of the meal just consumed, place his hands over his bloated belly, and say, "OK, this time I'm serious: I'm starting my diet tomorrow!" Tomorrow, of course, finds the leader waking up and devouring a large plate of leftover ham latkes with two poached eggs on top and a side of salty fried potatoes. The leader, caught in the act, is then expected to explain, "What, was I supposed to let it go to waste? I promise, once we run out of gefilte shrimp, the diet starts."

The Very Short Good-bye
at the Door

Following the example of the Wise Men, who bade the shepherds a brief farewell once Mary finally delivered the baby Jesus, the good-bye cannot take longer than 25 seconds—the amount of time it took for the Wise Men to grab the self-replenishing sheep stomach and the three remaining gifts, straighten their tunics, and get on their donkeys. Centuries later, Akiva Rosenblatt said the Wise Men's hasty departure should not be seen as an insult to the shepherds, who, by that time, had grown extremely ripe, but merely as a statement that sometimes you have to get a move on. Rosenblatt's paper, "Hit the Road, Magi: The Incontrovertible Evidence That the Wise Men's Departure Was Actually Not Hasty at All," changed forever what had been a tradition of having extremely long conversations and even making intricate plans "to get together sometime next week" while everyone had his coat on and half the group was already in the car outside.

CHAPTER 4

Chrismukkah in America:

One Family's Story

O dreidel, dreidel, dreidel
It spins with lots of torque
Right near the metal ladle
That serves creamed loin of pork
 —Traditional Chrismukkah song

AS THE HOLIDAYS arrive, the smallest thing—the sight of
a salt shaker, the "Day-Old Bialys, Half-Price" sign in
a bagel store window, the smell of a slacker's marijuana

joint—can jog the memory like one of Proust's beloved madeleines.

Growing up in Oak Park, Illinois, Moses Schmaltzberg's madeleine was the smell of potato latkes bubbling on the stove, the splattering grease leaving little stains on the stovetop. To him, the sight, the sound, and the smell always meant Hanukkah.

"For me, it just kicks the season into high gear," he told me. "If I smell a fried potato in March, it doesn't do anything for me, but when there's a bit of a chill in the air, that scent immediately reminds me of my Bubbie scraping potatoes over her old box grater, cutting herself, and then cursing in both Yiddish and English. When I was a boy, she used to let me beat an egg and mix in some matzo meal. And later, she'd let me scoop up the little shavings of potato and throw them into the egg mixture. Every year, she'd let me do a little more of the cooking, finally letting me drop the latkes into the hot oil when I was ten. And, eventually, she even taught me how to curse in Yiddish. Most of all, I remember the smell of those latkes sizzling in the pan. That smell always meant family and tradition to me."

For Britney Griffin, growing up in Birmingham, Alabama, family and tradition flooded her mind whenever she smelled her grandmother's oyster stuffing baking in the oven. "She used to serve it with extra mayonnaise, just like I liked," Britney told me. "And the Weavers would always bring over a loaf of Wonder Bread on Christmas morning so we could make sandwiches with the leftover pork and take them to Linn Park downtown for the annual Christmas parade!"

But when Moses and Britney married, their lives changed forever—and for the better, they both told me. "I guess we were both a little sheltered," Moses said. "Britney had never met a Jew before me—and I really didn't know much about Evangelical Christianity except what I

FAMOUS CHRISMUKKANS

Frida Kahlo

1907—1954

Mother: Matilde Calderon, a devout Catholic

Father: Guillermo Kahlo, a Jew of German descent

Known for: Figurative paintings/unibrow

Confused Religious Status: Championed female spirituality, yet had an affair with Leon Trotsky, a known atheist!

Fun Fact: Was not nearly as sexy in real life as Salma Hayek, who is *extremely* sexy!

read about Jim and Tammy Faye Bakker. It's been great, but there definitely have been some stresses. I think we've both learned that it's not so easy to share even your most beloved traditions with outsiders. But you know what? We're better now that we've found our own traditions. A ham latke is even better than a potato latke. I feel like now I'm getting the best of both worlds."

Britney plopped down on the couch next to Moses. "It wasn't so easy for me, either. My family was all about Christmas. It started right after Halloween, practically. Christmas this and Christmas that. My mother started buying presents in November, and she started planning her menu for Christmas dinner even before Thanksgiving—which is sort of ridiculous if you think about it, because Christmas dinner and Thanksgiving dinner are basically the same meal, right? I mean, how much turkey, stuffing, and pecan pie can you eat?!"

"Try telling your mother that!" Moses interjected, returning his attention to me. "For the first few years of our marriage, she demanded that we come to her house for Thanksgiving and for Christmas. And we went along for a while, but then we also had to go to my family for Hanukkah."

"Oy, vey," Britney added. "The tension! I remember that first Christmas dinner, when I brought Moses down to my parents' house in Birmingham. They tried to be polite, I guess, but just because Moses is Jewish doesn't mean you have to keep talking about how much you support Israel because the Jews are God's 'chosen people.' Every other word out of their mouths was 'chosen people.' I mean, come on! You should hear what they say about Jews when Moses isn't around!"

"I didn't really mind," Moses said. "I mean, think of all the effort it took to make that 12-pound ham roast—and to make sure it ended up right in front of my seat at the table!"

Britney continued: "Anyway, that was bad enough, but the whole time, my grammy kept looking at Moses's forehead. She wouldn't say nothin', but we knew she was looking for horns! So finally, Moses said, 'Grammy Griffin, Jews don't have horns anymore, you know. But if you want, I can show you my circumcision scar.' Well, her cheeks flushed brighter than a red velvet cake. It certainly shut everyone up for the rest of the night, let me tell you."

"We all sat there, and the only topic anyone would bring up was the weather!" Moses added. "We got through the meal, but it just wasn't any fun. I kept thinking, 'If only we were celebrating Chrismukkah, none of this would be happening. We'd be measuring the kids, singing monotone songs, and eating salty potatoes. No tension.'"

Moses said he actually felt worse when he brought Britney to his family's Hanukkah celebration. "Unlike Britney's parents, my parents didn't even try to be nice. I thought my father was making an effort when he said he wanted to invite Britney into the family by explaining to her what all the symbols of the holiday meant. So he's

Lindsey Vuolo

Born: Oct. 19, 1981

Mother: Russian Jew

Father: An Italian Catholic who converted to Judaism

Known for: 34 DD breasts

Confused Religious Status: Strips for money, yet still goes to temple.

Fun Fact: Lindsey is the only person to appear naked in *Playboy* with a caption containing the words, "My bat mitzvah..."

going around the table, pointing at things. 'Here's the menorah,' he said. 'It's a symbol of the sacred oil that Judah Maccabee burned after defeating the Syrian king Antiochus who had oppressed the Jews and tried to wipe us off the face of the earth! And here are the chocolate Hanukkah coins, which symbolize how Antiochus stole our money and made us beggars in our own land!' Man, my pop got so worked up that he started pointing out other symbols from other holidays. 'Here's a piece of horseradish! It symbolizes the bitterness of our slavery in Egypt, when the pharaohs oppressed and killed us. And this is a framed certificate I got from the Israeli government to show that I planted a tree in the Negev and helped reclaim the Holy Land from those Arab butchers! And this is a picture of me standing in front of the gates at Auschwitz, where the Germans killed hundreds of thousands of Jews in ovens and gas chambers! And here is a wheelchair—a symbol of Leon Klinghoffer, the guy who the Arabs threw off that cruise ship!' So I gently said to my father that maybe he should tone it down a bit. He went berserk! 'Tone it down? Tone it down? This is our history, Moses, or have you already forgotten it? People have been trying to kill us for centuries, and I just want your lovely wife to know about it.'"

Britney said she didn't blame Moshe Schmaltzberg. "He was only trying to welcome me into the family, I guess, although I did feel that he was trying to blame me for something. Moses's mom was nice, though."

"Nice?" Moses said. "She kept you in the kitchen the entire night."

"But she was teaching me how to cook your favorite foods, Moses," Britney said. "I had no idea you liked beef tongue so much!" (Moses later told me he ate beef tongue for a month after that before he finally summoned the courage to tell his new wife that, in fact, he detested beef tongue and that his mother had intentionally lied to her.)

For someone like myself, who has jetted all over the world for the past decade to research Chrismukkah traditions and rituals, Britney and Moses's experience was nothing new. I've heard from dozens of newly married Jews and Christians who can't believe the fault lines that suddenly get exposed during that first holiday season after the wedding. The happy couples knew of a holiday—Chrismukkah—that could end the tension that divides many families by giving them a single, unified, simple day to celebrate. And yet, Chrismukkah sometimes ended up creating even more tension.

But Moses and Britney had reached the tipping point and knew that celebrating Chrismukkah was the answer, a neutral ground where both families could come together and share some warmth without the tension of gift-giving, religious ceremonies, or constant reiteration that the story of Judaism is the story of 2,000 years of brutal human suffering. Their Chrismukkah wasn't meant to merely be a slapdash combination of their family traditions—no "Chrismukkah bush" here—but a way to bridge the chasm of misunderstanding between their two cultures.

There was the typical resistance at first from both families, with the Griffins and the Schmaltzbergs feigning ignorance at the holiday's traditions. "Your mom got so insulted when I took my Hour of Silent Reflection only ten minutes after she showed up," Moses said. "And I could tell she was really bothered when I refused to accept the gift she got me. Look, even if you don't follow the Chrismukkah tradition of automatic gift return, giving a Jew skin lotion because you think it will relieve the pain of circumcision is a weird present."

"Yeah, well, don't you remember when you burned all my father's argyle sweaters and said it was a Chrismukkah ritual?" Britney added.

"Well, they *were* green, weren't they?"

"Boy, was he mad!"

"Yes, but he learned about Chrismukkah, didn't he?"

Britney reminded Moses that her parents weren't the only relatives put off by the new Chrismukkah celebration.

"His mom came over with all of the food—a huge roasted chicken, noodle kugel, potato latkes, something called 'cholent,' which I swear I never saw anyone actually eat, and a boiled beef intestine—and kept saying, 'It's no bother, really, it's no bother.' But when I told her that we had made all the preparations and I showed her the salty fried potatoes and the roasted broccoli, she just said, 'You call this a holiday meal? And after I went through all this trouble?' She was bitter about it the whole night. She never even touched her day-old bialy!"

"The good news is that both families did observe one Chrismukkah ritual perfectly: the short goodbye at the door!" Moses laughed.

When Moses and Britney finally stopped inviting their families to the Chrismukkah celebration, they found themselves suddenly able to make the holiday their own. Moses devoted himself to understanding the ancient roots of Chrismukkah, diving into scholarly texts and weighing various interpretations. As a result, he and Britney tweaked many of the Chrismukkah rituals and foods.

"For a while, I was really inspired by Solomon the Wise Man's gift of the salt to Leah—a woman who looked so different from him and was so clearly outside his cultural and ethnic traditions," Moses said. "So one year, I took a box of kosher salt and walked around town throwing handfuls of salt at anyone who looked different from me."

"Until the police department arrested you and charged you with a hate crime," Britney said.

"It wasn't a hate crime! It was religious expression! But they were right, you can't go around throwing salt at people just because they're black or Hispanic. It was silly."

"So now we just leave bags of Lay's salt-and-vinegar potato chips at people's doors during the middle of the night," Britney said. "And when we go to someone's house for Christmas, we leave a tube of Pringles in their stockings. It's a way of sharing the tradition of Solomon's salt and Leah's potatoes, but also subtly mocking those traditions."

Moses and Britney even started hanging a metal spatula on their front door during the four days of Chrismukkah, a symbol of Leah and Solomon's first fried potato stand.

And even though Moses misses Hanukkah whenever he smells those fried potatoes, he has come to embrace the ham latkes that Britney makes every year. "They sure beat the 'filter fish' you used to eat," she said.

"That's *gefilte* fish, silly," Moses said, a gentle tone of reproach in his voice. "And besides, honey, we only eat gefilte fish during Eastover."

CHAPTER 5

Traditional Chrismukkah Recipes

There were some strange rituals, such as the Measuring of the Children, which I regarded as mere drollery, but then they brought out the feast! O Mary, what a feast it was! A heaping portion of salted potatoes, a great turkey, stale breadstuffs to chew, and such a wondrous dessert that they called "brownies." I felt in the bosom of all Humanity! Perhaps this Great War could be ended if we could get the rebels to simply join us at the Chrismukkah table.

—Abraham Lincoln,
letter to Mary Todd, January 2, 1862

I'VE ALWAYS BEEN DRAWN to chefs. What I really mean is that I've always been drawn to food, and chefs are merely along for the ride. But every Chrismukkah, I yearn for some of the classic holiday dishes my mother used to make. Unfortunately, my mother is a lousy cook, so what I really yearn for are the classic dishes prepared by someone other than my mother. And that's where chef Scott Campbell comes in.

Campbell, you see, is not only one of New York's top chefs, but he's also a practicing Chrismukkan, thanks to his marriage to his lovely wife, Linda. In fact, while most New York restaurants offer Christmas and Hanukkah meals, Campbell's Upper West Side eatery, @SQC., is the only restaurant in all of New York City that offers a complete Chrismukkah menu. It's available during the second half of December.

All of the recipes below are adapted from Campbell's once-a-year menu. "I call it Jewish nouvelle cuisine," Campbell told me. "What that means is that it's Jewish food cooked by a goy like me."

Chicken Soup with Pork-Fat Matzo Balls

For the soup:

1 chicken, cut up
1 bunch dill (not chopped)
1 bunch carrots, in big chunks
1 bunch celery, in big chunks
2 onions, quartered

For the matzo balls:

2 cups matzo meal
½ cup pork fat, rendered from bacon
1 cup seltzer
8 eggs
2 teaspoons salt

Place chicken pieces in large pot and fill with water until chicken is almost covered. Toss in dill, carrots, celery, and onions and boil for 2 hours. Remove all meat, bones, and disgusting parts. Strip meat off bones and set aside. Pour remaining liquid and vegetables through strainer. Retain veggies and chicken and refrigerate in their own bowl. Place soup in its own bowl, too, and refrigerate overnight. In the morning, scrape the chicken fat off the top of the soup and discard (or, if you're really gross like my grandparents, smear the fat onto crackers and die of arteriosclerosis when you're sixty—but don't say I didn't warn you!).

Mix matzo meal, pork fat, and seltzer. Whisk eggs in a separate bowl until frothy—not Oscar Wilde frothy, but Noel Coward frothy. Stir into matzo mixture and mix with salt. Refrigerate for 2 hours. Heat soup until warm, but not boiling. Scoop up some of the matzo mixture and form into balls. Not baseballs, but pool balls. (You should remember pool balls from the pool table you demanded your parents buy you for your eleventh birthday, but you never once used.) Place the balls in simmering soup. Cook for 35 minutes.

Savory Oyster Hamantaschen

For the dough:

2 cups flour, plus more for rolling out the dough

2 teaspoons baking powder

2/3 cup butter

1/3 cup sugar

2 eggs

Pinch salt

2 tablespoons milk

For the oyster filling:

¼ cup olive oil

1 onion, diced

2 cups red wine, preferably something undrinkable
   like Manischewitz

1 cup duck or turkey gravy

24 large oysters (I don't know what kind because I'm a Jew)

Sift together flour and baking powder in a large bowl. Set aside. In another large bowl, beat together butter, sugar, and one egg until fluffy. Add the flour mixture, beating until dough is formed. Gather dough into a ball and flatten. Cover in plastic wrap and place in refrigerator overnight.

When ready to use dough, preheat oven to 375 degrees F. Divide into two portions—equal portions, not like Israel and the West Bank—and roll both onto a lightly floured surface until about ¼-inch thick. Use a knife to cut as many triangles as possible. Take half of the triangles and cut out a smaller triangle from inside, so that there is a triangular-shaped hole in the center. Reroll all the cut out triangles so you don't waste dough, you waster, you! Place full triangles and cut triangles on a baking sheet. Beat remaining egg with milk in a small bowl. Brush mixture on the cut triangles. Bake all triangles for 15 to 20 minutes.

Heat oil on high. When the oil is hot but not smoking, add onion and cook until clear. Add wine to deglaze the pan. Bring to boil and add gravy. Again bring to a boil for 5 minutes. Reduce heat and place oysters into gravy and let cook for 30 seconds to 1 minute. Remove oysters and set aside. Continue allowing gravy to boil until it reduces by half. Remove from heat and stir oysters back into the sauce. Spoon the gravy mixture over the full triangles and cover with the cut triangles to simulate hamantaschen.

Gefilte Shrimp with Roasted Tomato and Horseradish Sauce

For the gefilte shrimp:
7 pounds shrimp, deveined (retain shells)
2 onions
2 medium carrots
3 large eggs
Freshly ground pepper to taste
1 cup matzo meal
6 cups shrimp stock

For the sauce:
3 tablespoons olive oil
3 cups chopped onion
3 cloves garlic, minced
3 pounds plum tomatoes, chopped
1/3 cup white vinegar

½ cup dark corn syrup
¼ teaspoon ground cloves
¼ teaspoon ground allspice
1 tablespoon salt
2 teaspoons freshly ground black pepper
⅓ cup horseradish, grated

If making your own shrimp stock (what are you, nuts?), place shrimp shells in 3 quarts of water and boil for 20 minutes. Strain and reserve.

To prepare the gefilte shrimp rolls, place the shrimp, onions, and carrots in the bowl of a food processor and process until no big lumps remain. Put in a large bowl. Add the eggs, one at a time, and the pepper and mix thoroughly. Stir in enough matzo meal to make a soft mixture that will hold its shape rather than being all wishy-washy like Hillary. Form into ovals about 3 inches long. Gently place the gefilte shrimp in the simmering stock. Cover and simmer for 20 to 30 minutes. When the gefilte shrimp is cooked, remove from the broth and allow to cool for at least 15 minutes.

To make the **Roasted Tomato and Horseradish Sauce**, heat the olive oil and cook the onion until golden brown, about 10 minutes. Add the garlic and cook for another minute. Add the tomatoes, vinegar, corn syrup, cloves, allspice, salt, and pepper. Boil, reduce heat, and simmer, stirring occasionally, for 1 hour. Strain the sauce into a bowl and return to the pot. Bring the sauce back to a simmer and cook until very thick, stirring

occasionally, about 45 minutes. Allow sauce to cool.
Add horseradish and refrigerate until needed.

Ham Latkes

1 pound Russet potatoes, grated

2 onions, shredded

3 eggs, beaten

½ cup matzo meal

2 teaspoons salt

2 teaspoons baking powder

1 pound ham, grated

Vegetable oil for frying

Place the potatoes and onions on thick paper towels over
a bowl to drain excess liquid. Set aside. In a large bowl,
combine the eggs, matzo meal, salt, and baking powder.
Stir in the ham, potatoes and onions. Heat vegetable oil
in a skillet over medium heat. Drop the latke mixture by
spoonfuls into the pan and flatten slightly. Turn only
once. Remove from the pan when latkes are crisp. Don't
do what I always do, which is test their doneness by putting one in my mouth. There's a reason the Inquisition
used to torture people with hot oil. Serve latkes warm
with apple sauce, sour cream, or—a new Chrismukkah
tradition—Dijon mustard.

Orange and Rosemary Turkey with Charoset-Andouille Stuffing

2 medium Granny Smith apples, peeled, cored, and chopped
½ pound walnuts, chopped
¼ cup honey
½ cup red wine, preferably something undrinkable
   like Manischewitz
1 stick butter
2 onions, sliced into rings
½ pound andouille sausage, cut into discs
3 matzos
1 turkey
20 cloves garlic, peeled
2 cups orange juice
Rosemary leaves, fresh or dried

In the bowl of a food processor, combine apples and walnuts. Pulse until well mixed but still coarse. Remove from food processor, put in a small bowl, and fold in the honey and the wine. Set aside. Heat butter in a saucepan. When the butter is hot but not yet browning, add onions and cook about 10 minutes, but do not burn. Stir in andouille discs and cook for two minutes. Remove from heat and pour into mixing bowl. Break up matzos and add to bowl, stirring to mix completely. Add apple-walnut mixture.

Preheat oven to 375 degrees F. Wash turkey and pat dry with paper towels. Place in roasting pan breast side up. (Yes, I know that many chefs are now cooking turkeys with the breast sides down, but like television, the miniskirt, and East Germany, this is a fad.) Insert garlic cloves into holes in skin and under seams, pinching and tugging to disperse evenly. Pour orange juice over turkey. Disperse rosemary leaves all over the place. Fill turkey cavity with stuffing mixture. Place into pre-heated oven and bake until done (if you have to ask how long that is, you need more than this recipe).

Charoset-Bourbon Noodle Kugel

2 medium Granny Smith apples, peeled, cored, and chopped
½ pound walnuts, chopped
½ cup bourbon
¼ cup honey
¾ pounds wide egg noodles, cooked
1 pound cottage cheese
1 cup sour cream
1 stick butter, melted
½ cup sugar
2 eggs, beaten
¾ cup raisins
Pinch of salt
Pinch of cinnamon
1 teaspoon vanilla extract

Preheat oven to 350 degrees F. In a food processor bowl, combine apples and walnuts. Pulse until well mixed but still coarse. Remove from food processor, put in a small bowl, and fold in bourbon and honey. Set aside. In a large mixing bowl, combine noodles and remaining ingredients and toss well. Add apple-walnut mixture. Transfer the entire mess to a buttered baking dish, and cook uncovered for a little more than 30 minutes. Remove. Reheat 30 minutes before serving and serve warm.

Chestnut Cranberry Rugelach

For the dough:

2 sticks butter, softened

8 ounces cream cheese, softened

3 cups flour, sifted

1/2 teaspoon salt

For filling:

8 ounces dried cranberries

1/2 cup chestnuts

1/2 cup granulated sugar

1/4 cup brown sugar, packed

1 teaspoon cinnamon

1/4 teaspoon vanilla

Confectioners' sugar for rolling out the dough

In a food processor, blend butter and cream cheese until smooth. Add flour and salt, and pulse just until mixture forms a ball. Form dough into a log. Chill dough, wrapped well in plastic wrap, at least 4 hours and up to I day.

To make the filling, chop cranberries and chestnuts, put in medium bowl, and mix in granulated sugar, brown sugar, cinnamon, and vanilla until well combined. Preheat oven to 350 degrees F.

Cut dough into eight pieces, but work with only one piece at a time (what's with you, got ADD?), keeping remaining pieces chilled. Sprinkle confectioners' sugar on the counter (you're such a mess), and roll out the dough into an 8-inch round. Sprinkle a small amount of the filling in a ring around outer portion of round, leaving a 1-inch border around edge, and press filling gently into dough. Fold outer edge of pastry over filling and roll up filling in pastry, jelly-roll fashion, folding sides under pastry to enclose filling. Transfer rugelach, as formed, pointed ends down, to ungreased baking sheets. Make more rugelach in same manner. Bake rugelach, rotating halfway through baking, until golden, typically 15 to 20 minutes. Transfer to cooling rack.

Mincemeat Sufganiyot Flambé

2 packages yeast

1 cup sugar

1 teaspoon salt

½ cup milk

½ cup melted butter

3 eggs, separated

3 ¾ cups flour

⅓ cup mincemeat filling (see absolutely crazy recipe below)
Vegetable oil for frying
1 cup bourbon

In a large bowl, dissolve the yeast in warm water and stir in ⅓ cup of the sugar and the salt. Add milk, butter, egg yolks, and two cups of the flour. Beat in the remaining flour until it forms a soft, smooth dough. Cover with a dish towel and let rise for about an hour or until it has doubled in size (or until the Messiah returns—just kidding!). Knead until it is elastic. Roll it out until it is ¼-inch thick. Cut with biscuit cutter into circles. Drop one teaspoon of mincemeat filling into center. Brush the edges of the circles with egg white, lay another circle on top and pinch together the edges to form a doughnut. Place all the doughnuts on a cookie sheet and let stand for an hour or so (too long for you? Get a hobby). Deep fry in vegetable oil. Do not drop sufganiyot into the oil. *Place* them into the hot oil with a spatula. Consider that a warning. Don't even think of suing me if you get burned. When ready to serve, place two sufganiyot on each person's plate and pour a small amount of bourbon on top. Stand back. Ignite. Again, don't sue me if you're clumsy with your bourbon. If you can't pour your bourbon cleanly, perhaps Chrismukkah isn't the holiday for you.

Mincemeat Filling

10 pounds pears
3 lemons, quartered and seeded (leave peel on)
1 ½ pounds ground beef
2 pounds raisins
1 teaspoon cinnamon
5 pounds brown sugar
1 tablespoon cider vinegar
1 teaspoon ground cloves
1 teaspoon allspice
1 cup bourbon
1 cup port wine

Peel and core enough pears to measure 4 quarts; place in bowl of food processor. Add lemons, and process lightly. Set aside. Cook ground beef in a large saucepan. Add pear-lemon mixture and remaining ingredients, mix well, and refrigerate for a week, checking to stir every few hours and, if necessary, replacing liquid. When ready to use, remove from fridge and bring to boil, stirring constantly. Use in whatever recipe you like (like the one above, silly).

Walnut Matzo Bûche de Nöel with Chocolate Butter Cream

¾ cup sugar

4 egg yolks

½ cup walnuts, ground

1 teaspoon vanilla

Zest of two lemons

4 egg whites

1 cup matzo meal

3 tablespoons lukewarm water

1 tablespoon dark rum

1 tablespoon sugar

1 cup heavy cream

3 cups chocolate buttercream (see recipe below)

Beat together sugar and egg yolks until frothy. Stir in walnuts, vanilla, and zest. In a separate bowl, beat egg whites until stiff. Fold into sugar-egg mixture. Stir in matzo meal and mix until firm. Line a cookie sheet with parchment paper. Butter and flour the parchment. Spread batter on cookie sheet and bake for 11 to 13 minutes. Place a floured piece of parchment on a counter and invert the baked cake onto it. Remove the parchment on the bottom to unstick and then place it back onto the cake. When barely lukewarm, roll cake and refrigerate.

Mix the water, rum, and sugar together. Set aside. Beat the heavy cream until stiff and combine with one cup of the chocolate buttercream. Set aside. Unroll the cake and remove the waxed paper on top. Brush with rum syrup and spread the creamy buttercream over the top. Carefully roll the cake up, removing the paper as you go. Spread the remaining chocolate cream all over the log and the ends. Pull the tines of a fork down the length of the log to simulate bark. If you want to get fancy, make some mushrooms out of marzipan. Put the whole thing in the refrigerator so it can set; otherwise, it'll drip all over the place and no one will believe the illusion that he is about to eat a mythical chocolate log.

Chocolate Buttercream

4 ounces bittersweet chocolate
2 ounces semisweet chocolate
²/₃ cup sugar
½ cup water
6 egg yolks
4 sticks butter, softened

Melt the chocolate in a small bowl and set aside. Mix the sugar and water in a small saucepan and bring to a boil for 2 minutes. Set aside and let cool. Place the egg yolks in a mixer and pour the cooled sugar syrup over the top.

Beat at high speed for 5 minutes, or until the mixture is thick and pale yellow. Add the butter bit by bit, mixing at low to medium speed until smooth. Mix in the melted chocolate, beating until smooth.

Smoked Ham and Cheddar Matzo Brei Omelet

4 tablespoons butter
2 large onions, diced
3 matzos, broken up
8 eggs, beaten
1 ½ cups diced ham
½ cup cheddar cheese, shredded
Salt and pepper to taste

Heat the butter in a sauté pan until warm but not smoking. Add onions and cook slowly until translucent but not brown, approximately 15 to 20 minutes. Soak matzo pieces in eggs for 30 seconds and remove. Pour matzo and eggs into pan and add ham. Cook until eggs solidify. Turn off heat and fold in cheddar cheese until it melts. Add salt and pepper. Serve immediately.

Winona Ryder

Born: Oct. 29, 1971

Mother: Cindy Palmer, English

Father: Michael Horowitz, Brooklyn Jew

Known for: Wispy acting roles/shoplifting

Confused Religious Status: Born Winona Laura Horowitz, she picked her surname because her dad's Mitch Ryder album was playing when director David Seltzer asked how she should be credited.

Fun Fact: Winona has a brother named Yuri and half siblings named Jubal and Sunyata!

CHAPTER 6

ETHAN'S FIRST CHRISMUKKAH:

A Children's Book

By Thurston Mandelbaum-Summers

Ethan Howell-Epstein never liked December. His cousin on his mother's side, Muffy Howell, celebrated a holiday called Christmas, while his cousin on his father's side, Moshe Epstein, celebrated something called Hanukkah. Every year, Ethan and his parents either flew to Colorado Springs to be with the Howells or drove to Brooklyn to celebrate with the Epsteins.

But this year Ethan's father, Schmuel, said, enough.

"Enough!" he cried. "This year, everyone is going to come to *our* house!"

"But, Dad," Ethan said, "we don't even have a holiday."

Ethan's father sat him down. "Listen, Ethan," he said. "Your mother and I never told you, but we *do* have a holiday. It's called 'Chrismukkah'—and it's the best holiday in the world!"

"But why haven't we ever celebrated it?" Ethan asked.

"Look, Ethan, there are some things you don't understand—responsibility, family logistics, guilt—and I promise to explain them all to you someday, but we've got to get this house ready for Chrismukkah!"

"Yay!" Ethan yelled, and he rushed out to the garage with his father to get the shovels, while his mother, Ginger, started making salty fried potatoes.

When the big day came, Muffy and Moshe were confused. "Where is the tree? What's this?" Muffy asked, pointing to the mound of dirt in the living room.

"That's the Mound of Remembrance," Ethan said excitedly. "It's where we sit and reflect during the Reading of the Four Short, Easy-to-Remember Directives."

"But where is the menorah? Is this it?" Moshe asked, grabbing the dried gourd off the shelf.

Ethan's father came into the room just then and took the gourd from Moshe. "No, Moshe, that's the Sacred Vessel. It commemorates the Miracle of the Replenishing Herb."

Ethan's father heard a car door slam in the driveway and looked outside to see Grammy Howell and Bubbie Esther walking up the path. He grabbed the vessel from Moshe and headed to the basement.

"I'll take that, Cousin Moshe. Now, if you'll excuse me . . ."

The doorbell rang, and Grammy Howell and Bubbie Esther entered—and their arms were loaded down with several large packages.

"Grammy!" screamed Molly.

"Bubbie!" screamed Moshe.

"What have you brought us?!" they screamed in unison.

"In a minute! In a minute!" Grammy said. "Ethan, where is your father?"

"You just missed him," Ethan said. "He's having his Hour of Silent Reflection!"

"And your mother?" asked Bubbie.

"She's making gefilte ham and matzo-meal fruitcake," Ethan answered. "They're also Chrismukkah traditions!"

Grammy and Bubbie were proud of Ethan's excitement. But they still had gifts to give out. Molly got the Miss Moppet doll she wanted, and Moshe got the new Mega-Powers action figures.

But for Ethan, both grandmothers thought they had the perfect gift.

"Here, Ethan," Grammy said. "Your bubbie and I picked this out just for you!"

It was a new bicycle! And it was exactly what Ethan wanted! It had ten speeds, a banana-shaped seat, and thick off-road tires! Ethan couldn't wait to show his friends.

"Nu?" asked Bubbie.

"So, what do you think?" asked Grammy.

Ethan suddenly remembered that this was
Chrismukkah and what his father told him about
how important it was to the Howell-Epsteins
to have a holiday all their own. So Ethan knew
that he had to do.

"Grammy. Bubbie. Thank you for the bicycle, but
as the shepherd Ezekiel once said, 'I have no use
for this, so please take it away.' I'm paraphrasing,
of course."

Just then, Ethan's father emerged from the
basement.

"You did it, Ethan! I'm so proud of you," he said.

"But Dad, I really wanted that bicycle," Ethan
whispered.

"But you got something better! You got a holiday
you'll have for the rest of your life. You got
your first Chrismukkah—the best Chrismukkah
ever!"

It was the first and best Chrismukkah for Molly
and Moshe too. And they spent the rest of the day
riding around on the new bicycle.

CHAPTER 7

Found!
Dickens's Long-Lost
First Draft of
A Chrismukkah Carol

MY RESEARCH *for* Chrismukkah *took me all over the world—
to the Holy Land, to Rome, to Amsterdam (well, that research wasn't
entirely book-related). During a fact-finding mission in London, I was
rooting around the sub-basement of a museum when I uncovered
some handwritten notes that I later determined were the first draft of
Charles Dickens's unpublished classic,* A Chrismukkah Carol.
Further research showed that Dickens himself considered the book his most

promising but that he abandoned it in disgust when his publisher demanded that the story center on a trendier holiday called "Christmas."

MARLEY WAS DEAD. And so was Blitzstein. Of that there could be no doubt. Marley had died after eating a particularly large pheasant cooked a delightfully rich sauce that turned out to be rancid. Blitzstein succumbed after tripping on a Dutch cobblestone in Camden Town, shattering his knee and sending a small bit of marrow directly to his heart. Scrooge himself had signed the death certificates. Marley and Blitzstein were dead as doornails.

A word about Mr. Ebenezer Scrooge. All of London knew Scrooge as a tightfisted old fezzitwaddledinger. His heart was as cold as the limestone walkway of Edinburgh Castle in January, and his features were nipped and shriveled from the frost within. Even on the hottest day of summer, a shiver would emanate from anyone who encountered Scrooge on the street, so cold was his countenance, so tightly held his fists, so rigid his gait. And he didn't thaw one degree during Chrismukkah.

The less contact with the warmth of humanity, the better. "Keep your distance," he bade, "away with thee. I have money to count—and, truth be told, I have yet to figure out Old Blitzstein's filing system."

The counting would continue every day, 365 days a year, without a break. Even on the eve of Chrismukkah, when the candles in all the other offices had been extinguished and the workers therein were rushing to procure their Chrismukkah bialys and gifts that would never be accepted, Scrooge would sit over his files and numbers and continue the count.

One day, the door of the counting house opened and his nephew stood in the entryway.

"Joyous Chrismukkah, Uncle!" the nephew said.

"Chrismukkah, bumhug!" Scrooge said.

"Bumhug?" the nephew asked.

"I'm trying out new words to dismiss dim-witted fools like you," Scrooge explained. "Bear with me. I've tried 'Gubmuh!' Tried 'Buhmug!' I've even tried 'Mubguh!' But nothing seems to work."

"How about 'Humbug!'" his nephew offered cheerfully.

"Humbug! Spot on, Nephew. Now, begone with you: Humbug!"

"Pray, dear uncle, what have you against Chrismukkah? I understand that you have always had a problem with Christmas, with its emphasis on joy, presents, and goodwill toward the less fortunate, but Chrismukkah concerns itself with none of those things. Why does it tax you so?"

"For one thing, I find it inefficient—this purchasing of gifts that will not be accepted. Why not skip the entire thing and merely *say* that you have bought the present? I also disapprove of the waste of perfectly good day-old bialys. Do you know that I am consuming bialys as old as two weeks!"

"Uncle, you cannot mean that!"

"What, pray, has Chrismukkah done for you, Nephew?"

"Is that a rhetorical question, Uncle?"

"Yes. Begone with you, Nephew!"

"Damn your sophistry, Uncle. Please come to our Chrismukkah feast tomorrow. Hadassah has procured some particularly pleasing 'broccoli rabe' from the 'produce man.' I believe you are a man, Uncle, who could benefit from that particular Chrismukkah ritual."

"Bah, humbug! Yes, Nephew, thanks for your help with that word. It really is perfect. Now, good day, sir!"

"Joyous Chrismukkah, Uncle."

"I said, 'Good *day!*'"

Scrooge's nephew finally withdrew, but the idiot opened the door just as two other fools were approaching.

"Joyous Chrismukkah, Mr. Scrooge!" one said. "At this time of year, it is often desirable to make a small donation to provide destitute Chrismukkans with food, drink, and hallucinogenic drugs. Otherwise, they will go without."

"Are there no Amsterdam-style coffee houses where they can indenture themselves?"

"Why, yes, Mr. Scrooge, but—"

"And the bagel stores? Do they not have Dumpsters into which they throw day-old bialys?"

"Yes, Mr. Scrooge, but I wish it were not true."

"Well I, for one, am glad to hear it! That is where I choose to make my contribution—through the purchase of my own drugs and my own bialys, friend."

"But this is Chrismukkah, sir. A season when all men of good faith are in celebration. Is a single pound too much to ask, that we may at least purchase gifts that will not be accepted? What shall we put you down for?"

"Nothing," Scrooge said.

"Ah, you wish to be anonymous?" the man asked.

"I wish to be left alone! I shall not assist the idle and indigent. If they do not wish to sign a seven-year indenture at a coffeehouse, why should I assist their sloth? Now, good day, gentlemen."

The men saw that it was no use and withdrew. Alas, Scrooge's poor clerk now warily approached the old man. Scrooge anticipated the request.

"I suppose you'll want the whole day, then?"

"It *is* Chrismukkah, sir."

"Chrismukkah, bah humbug! First the Christians want a day off for Christmas. And then the Jews want eight days off for Hanukkah. Now I hear that even the slaves will want a day off for this Kwanzaa holiday. When will it end?"

The clerk promised that he would make up for it by arriving a half hour early every day for the next month— but, alas, he had an additional request.

"Mr. Scrooge, sir? Are you going to eat the rest of that bialy?"

"This bialy? I may. I may not."

"Well, if you're going to eat it, of course, sir, eat it. I was just thinking—"

"I know what you were thinking, clerk. But if I choose not to eat this bialy, into the dustbin it will go. It will not grace your Chrismukkah table on the morrow. If you want a day-old bialy, you must procure it yourself. Begone with thee!"

Scrooge took his melancholy dinner at his usual melancholy tavern, went home, and climbed into bed with his banker's book. Without warning, the bell over his fireplace began to toll, softly at first, but then wildly, clanging to and fro with great speed and noise. And just as quickly, it stopped, replaced by the sound of chains scraping against the wood floor.

"Humbug!" Scrooge said. "Who is there?"

"It is we, Ebenezer!"

"We? Who 'we'? Is that even grammatical?"

Two apparitions suddenly appeared at the foot of Scrooge's bed.

"Marley! Blitzstein! Why, pray, what are you doing here?"

"I'm here to warn you, my dear old partner," Marley's ghost said.

"And I'm here because it sounded like fun. I mean, I get so bored," added the ghost of Blitzstein.

"*You* get bored! I have to walk the earth, all day and night, and you get bored," Marley's ghost said, unraveling one of the heavy chains across his chest and wrapping it around Blitzstein's head, choking him. Blitzstein removed his gangrenous right leg and hit Marley over the head with it.

"Fellas, fellas," Scrooge said at last. "Can somebody tell me what's going on here?"

"Oh, yeah, I forgot. Truth is, we have a message for you, Scrooge," Marley said.

"Humbug!" Scrooge said.

"You're really liking that word, aren't you?" Blitzstein said.

Just then, Marley's ghost unwrapped the bandages from his head, letting his jaw fall onto his chest.

"O horrors!" Scrooge exclaimed.

And Blitzstein's ghost unwrapped the bandages around his waistcoat and withdrew the entirety of his intestinal tract, held it like a lasso, tossed it over Scrooge's head, and pulled the slack taut.

"Oh, now that's just gross!" Scrooge complained.

"Sorry, bit of ghost humor. Scared enough to listen to us yet?"

"Yes. But what do you want of me?"

"Do you see these chains, Scrooge?" Marley asked. "They are the iron links I forged in life. Rather than allow my spirit to wander, I kept it confined in the office of the counting house. And now I must walk the earth forever."

"That doesn't sound fair," Scrooge said.

"You're telling me!"

"No, what I mean is, your punishment should be that you're confined to the counting house all day and night, not that you are forced to travel the earth. See what I mean? The punishment should fit the offense."

"Look, it's bad enough I have to walk the earth with these chains, and this guy is saying it's not the right punishment. You know what, Scrooge, why don't you write that down and shove it into your suggestion slot?"

"But, pray, Marley, you were always such a good man of business," Scrooge said.

"Business?! Scrooge, my business was the business of mankind! But I ignored my fellow man for the short-sighted goal of financial gain!"

"And you, Blitzstein, you were the opposite of Marley, always with a laugh and quick to help a man in need."

"All true, dear Scrooge, but do you see this gangrenous leg?" Blitzstein asked. "Well, I was a bit too eager to laugh or help my fellow man, perhaps. Picked up a touch of the clap during that 'business trip' to Paris in '36. So, from Marley, you're learning that the spirit needs to be unfettered, but from me, you learn that you really should use condoms when going to a brothel on the Left Bank. What was I thinking?!"

"I *knew* that trip was a boondoggle!" Scrooge said. "We didn't even have an account in Paris!"

"Can we get on with this? I have to be in Manchester later. It's a long walk, as you might imagine," Marley said.

"Yeah, OK," Blitzstein said. "Look, Scrooge, we have some bad news for you. Tonight, you're going to be visited by three ghosts: the Ghost of Chrismukkah Past, the Ghost of Chrismukkah Present, and the Ghost of Chrismukkah Yet to Come."

"Hmm, that is bad news," Scrooge said. "OK, so what's the good news?"

"Who said anything about *good* news?" Marley replied.

"Good one," said Blitzstein. "You still got it, Marley!" And the pair of ghosts withdrew.

"OK, that was weird," Scrooge said, falling asleep so quickly and deeply that he failed to remove his clothing.

Scrooge had no idea how much time had passed when he was awakened by the first apparition, childlike in its features. "Are you that ghost Marley told me about?" he asked.

"That's me, pal," the ghost said, sticking out his hand. "Ghost of Chrismukkah Past. Look, we've got a lot to see tonight, so if you don't mind…" The apparition grasped Scrooge's hand and led him through the open window, up over London to a small town about 4 miles away. "I know this place!" Scrooge said. "I was born here. Look below! That is the street on which I lived."

"Are you the tour guide, or am I?" the spirit said sarcastically. "But if you know the place so well, I'm sure you won't be surprised by what we'll see down here."

The spirit and Scrooge descended toward a boarding school, completely empty.

"My old school! But, pray, where is everyone?"

"Alas, Scrooge, they are all home for Chrismukkah— but the building is not entirely empty, is it?"

The spirit pointed down to a single room illuminated by one flickering candle. Inside, a quiet boy—a solitary figure!—sat reading. Scrooge looked down and saw that it was his own forgotten self, as a sorry boy.

"This is how he spent his Chrismukkah every year—alone, reading, while all others were making mirth and smoking hashish," the spirit said. "Let's go. I've got something else to show you. Remember this place?"

By now, Scrooge and the ghost had flown back over to London and were descending on a warehouse. "Of course; I was apprenticed here," Scrooge said. "Why, there's Old Fezziwig, alive again. It warms the heart to see him again."

The ghost and Scrooge took a position near the back of the room. Suddenly, the clock struck seven and Fezziwig clapped his hands. "Ebenezer! No more work today." As Scrooge cleared the room of furniture, Mrs. Fezziwig entered, bearing a great cold roast. Behind her were several Miss Fezziwigs bearing mince pies, cold beer, and a piece of cold boiled. And behind them were some of the many suitors who had failed to win their hearts. And behind the suitors were some friends of friends who had crashed the party after hearing there would be cold boiled. And there was also a fiddler who struck up his tune, "My Lift Has a Lorry in the Boot on Chrismukkah Day!" And, oh, the dancing! Old Fezziwig and Mrs. Fezziwig cut quite a figure, spinning, turning, doing the "Queen Victoria" and the "Lumbroodle." Scrooge himself danced with several of the Miss Fezziwigs and took quite a shine to Amy Fezziwig, who possessed a face that seemed to be configured for kissing and a set of hips that gave Scrooge a flushed fever just to contemplate.

At long last, he summoned up the courage and asked, "Miss Fezziwig, pray tell, what kind of name *is* Fezziwig anyway?"

"Why, it is a Chrismukkan surname, Mr. Scrooge, why do you ask?"

"I was just thinking, er, never mind."

The Ghost of Chrismukkahs Past pointed to the younger Scrooge and Miss Fezziwig dancing. "Idiot! What were you thinking, fool? You could have had her faster than you could say, 'Do you have Prince Albert in a can?'!"

"I was raised Jewish, but my mother was a Christian," Scrooge explained. "Yet we never celebrated Chrismukkah like the Fezziwigs. I guess I blew it. O what sorrow! What sadness!"

"Sorry, pal, but it gets worse," the spirit said, and he and Scrooge flew into a happy home where an attractive woman and her husband sat on the couch, their legs intertwined. "My love, I ran into an acquaintance of yours this afternoon, a Mr. Scrooge, I believe he was named. What a horrible, sad creature."

"I knew him once, true, dear husband, but he missed his chance. He could have had this," the woman said, ripping open her blouse and pulling her husband toward her. The man ravished his wife, who returned his favors in kind. And, dear reader, rather wantonly. The heart pounds to think of it even today.

"Spirit! Pray tell, who is this woman?" Scrooge asked.

"Why, Scrooge, are you dim? That is Amy Fezziwig, of course."

"Enough, great spirit! Take me away. This one I cannot bear."

"Actually, I kinda wish we could watch a bit more. It's just getting good. They're really getting into it. Ooh, baby, check it out. I'm going to have to alert Mr. Guinness about these two for his book."

"No, spirit, get me out of here and back to my cold, lonely bed. I have seen too much tonight. Haunt me no longer!"

"As you wish," and the spirit vaporized, leaving Scrooge exactly where he started, alone in his bed, where he fell promptly asleep.

Not five minutes passed when the second of the apparitions nudged Scrooge awake.

"Sorry, buddy, but wake up," the spirit said.

"Are you the Ghost of Chrismukkah Present?"

"That's me, hooknose, but we gotta go. You're not the only curmudgeon on my list tonight." The spirit carried Scrooge over the city toward Camden Town and through the living room window of one particularly dreary home. Yet no one inside was dreary at all. Inside, Mrs. Cratchit prepared the Chrismukkah feast and Master Peter peeled potatoes, while two younger Cratchits, a girl and a boy, ran about, dreaming of their mother's gefilte clams, bacon-wrapped chicken liver, savory oyster hamantaschen, and charoset kugel, though there was only enough for a bite or two per person. Just then, Martha Cratchit entered, and her father behind her with Tiny Tim borne aloft on his shoulders, Tim's cane and metal leg braces dangling behind him.

"Spirit, tell me," Scrooge asked. "Did Bob and Tim manage to procure the sacred Chrismukkah herb?"

"Are there no Amsterdam-style coffee houses where they could indenture themselves?" the Spirit asked. It pained Scrooge to hear himself quoted, albeit accurately, back to himself.

"And, Spirit, tell me, did Bob Cratchit even get a day-old bialy for his Chrismukkah table?"

"Was there no Dumpster into which Tiny Tim could dive?"

"Ease up, Spirit," Scrooge said, pained by the paraphrase. "You're taking me a bit out of context, you know."

"I think it's fair, given the circumstances. Alas, now I must go, but you should remember what you saw here today," the Spirit said, and dissolved into the smoke of the smoldering wood in Scrooge's unhappy fireplace.

At last, Scrooge fell asleep again but was promptly awakened by the third apparition of the night. He awoke to the sight of a bony finger in his face. The finger led to a bony arm that disappeared under a black cloak, illuminated from within only by two glowing pieces of coal.

"Are you the third spirit that was mentioned to me?" Scrooge asked.

This spirit, however, did not speak, but merely beckoned Scrooge by crooking its finger.

"I'll come with you, but what's with the silent treatment? I understand that you are here to do me good but can't we exchange pleasantries while we go?"

The spirit responded only by pointing out the window at a group of businessmen discussing the death of a colleague.

"Please, Mr. Yingelburt, the undertaker says we need but five more pallbearers," one of the men, who was stately plump, said.

"I wouldn't carry Ebenezer Scrooge's dead body to the cemetery if you paid me!" the other man, who was just as plump, said.

"There'll be a lunch buffet!"

"I'm there! But, pray tell me, how is it possible that Scrooge paid for a lunch buffet for his pallbearers? This is a man who, in life, would take a tuppence from a sleeping beggar! He would sell worthless swampland to a widow! He would steal the gold tooth out of a consumptive!"

"Ah, 'tis true—but Scrooge himself did not pay for the buffet, at least not directly, that is! Scrooge had asked the undertaker to bury him in a fine mahogany casket. But the undertaker put Scrooge in a cardboard box and used the money for the buffet. And what a buffet! A cold roast and jellied venison! So, shall we go?"

The spirit pointed at the men. Scrooge understood.

"Well, clearly, I should have been nicer to people, so that they wouldn't have to be bribed to carry my lifeless corpse," Scrooge admitted. "But the real lesson you learn is, don't pay for a fancy burial. O great spirit, can you show me some tenderness in death?"

The spirit carried Scrooge over the city to Camden Town and to the home of his clerk, Bob Cratchit. Inside the sparse living quarters, the family was grieving over the death of Tiny Tim. Scrooge went ashen.

"If I had only provided the leftover bialy, perhaps Tiny Tim would have lived! O spirit, I have wronged my clerk, Bob Cratchit! Take me away, I cannot bear it."

The spirit was agreeable to this request, as there was one place remaining to visit. The pair flew over the churchyard and into the cemetery, soaring past the rows and rows of tombstones—there's Old Fezziwig! There's Mr. Grumbledrook, my first teacher! There's Mrs. Pulchyumbordum, my father's secretary, the one I secretly wanted to play Hide the Spotted Dick with!—before coasting to a stop at a cracked and soiled grave marker. Again the bony finger of the spirit pointed, and Scrooge followed with his eyes from the decayed fingernail to the tombstone.

EBENEZER SCROOGE, 1759–1839.
A man of business.

"O horrors! 'A man of business'? That's all they could think of writing?"

The spirit held out his bony arms, to suggest a complete lack of culpability.

"Oh, now I recall, spirit! I asked for that inscription myself, six years ago when I prepared my funereal affairs! The undertaker had suggested 'Have a nice day,' but I refused. I thought 'A man of business' captured who I was—and now I see, alas, O great spirit, that I was all too right. Take me back, take me back!"

Scrooge kept screaming and eventually woke up in his own bed, still muttering the words from his dream. When he awakened, Scrooge was a changed man. "All three spirits shall live through me this Chrismukkah! I shall keep Chrismukkah in my heart all year long!" He ran out into the street and grabbed the first boy he could find.

"Oy, you there, young boy! Do you know the bagelman, round in High Street?"

"I should hope so, sir!"

"A remarkable boy!" Scrooge said. "What a pleasure to talk to him! Well, young sir, have they opened for the morning yet?"

"What, the bagelman?"

"I love this kid! Fantastic. Yes, young sir, the bagelman. Has he opened for the morning?"

"Just opened."

"Good, good. Here, take this half crown and tell the bagelman you want to buy all of his day-old bialys!"

"Oy, day-olds?! For this money, you could have his entire larder of fresh ones!"

"A delightful boy! I shall have to remember to talk to him again. Yes, I know that, young sir, but please, bring all the day-olds to Bob Cratchit's house in Camden Town."

"Camden Town? Um, that's a bit far, you know."

"What a pleasure to talk to this kid! Yes, I get your hint. Here's another half crown to hire a cab. Now, go! Go! Get those old bialys to Bob Cratchit!"

The boy sped off in the direction of the bagel store. Just then, Scrooge spied another boy shuffling past, a nervous-looking lad with a cap pulled down low over his head, the kind of boy whom Scrooge had always endeavored to avoid in the past for fear that he was involved in nefarious trading.

"You there! Boy! Do you know where I can procure some narcotics?"

"Eh? Narcotics? Whatcha mean, guv'ner?"

"Oh, these children, I can't get enough of them today! You know, son, a little leafy material for my pipe, eh? Eh? Get my drift?"

"I have no idea whatcha mean, guv'ner."

"Perhaps this will refresh your memory, young lad," Scrooge said, producing from his pocket a prodigious bankroll of pound notes. He peeled off a five-pound note and gave it to the lad. "Now, go get me six ounces of your best weed at once—and keep a half crown for yourself."

"Now you're talking, guv'ner."

Scrooge rushed upstairs, made his toilet, and got dressed. By the time he got back, the lad was back with the hallucinogens. Scrooge pocketed the envelope and ran, practically dancing, to Camden Town. He peered in to the sparse living room and saw that the bialys had already arrived. The Cratchits had gathered around the bundle and were chewing away mercilessly, finally spitting out the bialys and laughing! Just then, Scrooge entered.

"Mr. Scrooge! Mr. Scrooge," Bob Cratchit said. "Welcome."

"I know I have not always been good to you, Bob, but I promise I have changed. In other words, 'Joyous Chrismukkah to all!'"

And then Scrooge slipped Bob Cratchit the envelope filled with the Chrismukkah herb.

"Golly, Mr. Scrooge! Bless us all, every one!"

Kevin Kline

Born: Oct. 24, 1947

Mother: Irish Catholic

Father: Jewish

Known for: Theatrical roles

Confused Religious Status: Raised catholic but made his fame working with many Jewish directors on Broadway.

Fun Fact: Kevin turns down so many roles that his nickname in the business is "Kevin Decline"!

CHAPTER 8

The Future
of
Chrismukkah

*"With our new line of Chrismukkah cards, wrapping paper,
and gift items, followers can share their love this season just
like people who celebrate Christmas, Hanukkah, and the
Wiccan holiday Imbolc. Middleton: Filling the World with
Pablum Since 1910."*

**—Middleton Greeting Card
Company press release**

DAVENPORT, IOWA, APRIL 2006—Dan Spector is a man on a mission. As the Middleton Company's vice president of new holiday exploitation, Spector, 56, is in charge of what the company hopes will be its most successful new holiday launch since Middleton turned the obscure Islamic holiday Eid al-Fitr into America's third-most-popular celebration, behind only Christmas and Columbus Day. But this is the Big One for Middleton, a 125-year-old company that was once the nation's foremost greeting card maker yet has struggled as its main competitor, Hallmark, has captured more market share every year.

Middleton executives have thrown all of the company's remaining resources into a last-ditch effort to beat Hallmark to the Chrismukkah market, but it's already mid-April, so Spector has no time to suffer fools gladly. Sure, he still has eight months before Chrismukkah, but Spector is accustomed to having two years before rolling out a new line of holiday cards, gifts, and decorations—and, most important, creating an entire mythological back story so that all the merchandise makes sense. He certainly doesn't want a repeat of the company's infamous Flag Day debacle. It started out so promisingly when Spector's former boss came up with the bright idea of teaming the celebration with an animated character called "The Flame of Freedom," who resembled a cross between a teddy bear and the Statue of Liberty. Everyone loved the cuddly character, of course—until an 8-year-old playing with the "Flame" at the live-action show on the National Mall in Washington, DC, accidentally dropped his torch and set fire to six pallets of giveaway American flags. By the time the fire was extinguished, part of the Smithsonian Institution had been burned to the ground, and Supreme Court Justice David Souter had been taken to Walter Reed Hospital with minor smoke inhalation. After a Congressional investigation, several Middleton executives were indicted and fired, paving the way for Spector to take over the Exploitation office.

Chrismukkah is Spector's first assignment, which explains why he's a bit eager to hit the ground running. Already on his fourth cup of coffee—it's 9:30 in the morning—Spector has gathered the company's best artists to review their preliminary designs. He's been in these kinds of sessions before and knows what to expect.

"I'm not looking for every one of the guys to hit the ball out of the park," Spector tells me. "A few doubles, maybe a triple would be nice, but when you're designing greeting cards to make America happy, all I need is a few clean singles. Every time I get involved in a new project, I remind myself what our founder, J. G. Middleton, always said: 'Give the people what they want. And if they don't want it, dumb it down a bit more and then give it to them again.' He is still such an inspiration to me, that J. G. Middleton."

While waiting for the artists to saunter in—9:30 is clearly early for this particular portion of the Middleton workforce—Spector tells me a story of a similar gathering he convened when the company put him in charge of Holiday Revitalization.

The Holiday Revitalization Task Force

We had to come up with an entirely new concept for Easter—in six weeks, start to finish, a complete overhaul of one of the world's beloved holidays!" Spector says, a bit of sugar from his powdered doughnut falling onto his Middleton "Peanuts Gang" tie. "So the artists come in, and I'm thinking, 'Please, just give me one card—one card!—I can use. Just one. I'm sitting there, and the artists are showing me their mock-ups, one by one. The first guy—I'll never forget this—shows me a sketch of a ghostlike Jesus rising off a cross toward the heavens. And inside, the inscription reads, 'Don't feel guilty. This whole thing was my idea.' And then the next guy comes over with his mock-up. It's Jesus Christ up in Heaven sitting poolside with Ramses II,—you know, the most brutal pharaoh of them all, a man believed to be one of the most heinous figures in the history of the world, pre-Christ at least. And Jesus just leans over and says, 'After you, we tightened the admission requirements.' At that point, I didn't need to see anything else! I threw them all out of here. Damn it, everyone wants to write for the fucking *Daily Show!* But when you're doing greeting cards, it has to be something you could send to your grandmother in Davenport. Well, we're in Davenport right now, but you get the idea. I ended up getting only a single new Easter card from that entire Revitalization: It was a picture of Jesus holding a can of beer and toasting the cardholder. Inside, the caption said, 'This afterlife's for you!'" Spector paused before saying, "I know, not even a double. But it worked. And compared to that, Chrismukkah is a cakewalk."

The artists started filing in, a bit sheepishly. Spector had warned me that greeting card artists are a notoriously insecure, underappreciated bunch, a classic group of misunderstood poets who think they should be writing anthologies of verse that will be remembered forever, not four-line stanzas that will find their final resting place under a magnet on a grandmother's refrigerator door. One of Middleton's card writers, Richard Sifuentes, even won the Pulitzer Prize for Poetry in 1984 for writing *Hope Springs Eternal, So You'd Better Bring a Slicker and Other Poems*, but the entire print run netted only $21.45 in royalties, so Sifuentes was back at his Middleton drafting table even while holding down the post of Poet Laureate of the United States for two consecutive years. "None of them can make a living as poets," Spector laughs. "But the cruelty of the marketplace is my good fortune, I guess. I'd be in real trouble if this country actually respected poets. If a real poet could earn five or six fig-ures—or even four—I don't know where I'd get my card writers."

Spector knows that when a deadline is just a few months away, he has to employ a businesslike approach, rather than an appeal to the artists' creativity. "So, what have you got for me?" he barks, and the meeting falls into what is clearly a familiar pattern. Winston Lamonte, whose 41 years at the company make him the senior art-ist present, goes first. His sketch, while not complete, conveys its idea immediately: On the cover, the Eas-ter Bunny, Judah Maccabee, King David, Ebenezer Scrooge, a Roman centurion, and Rudolph the Red-Nosed Reindeer are all on line at the unemployment office. Jesus is at the head of the line, listening to the clerk, while a teary Santa Claus is walking away from the window. Inside, the caption reads, "It's like I told that guy in the red suit—it's probably just a Chrismukkah-week downsize. You'll be back on your feet in no time."

Lamonte's fellow artists all crack up, but Spector is not completely pleased. "I love the setup," he said. "I love that all the Hanukkah and Christmas icons are unem-ployed. I even love that you threw in the Easter Bunny. It's funny, and it also sets up our forthcoming line of Eastover cards. I really do love it. Jesus at the unemploy-ment line! It's irreverent without being tasteless." After a pause, he said, "Well, it is tasteless, but I still like it. OK, let's get rid of Jesus. Can we just have Santa and the other guys on the unemployment line? Otherwise, you know, we are actually saying that the son of God can't find a job. Now, there's also something about that caption. It's just too wordy. Can't it just be, 'Chrismukkah, buddy. You understand.' Something simple, you know? The second you mention "downsize," you have about a million Americans start worrying about their own jobs. And I can't sell Chrismukkah cards to people who think they're about to lose their jobs. Yeah, come to think of it, this card isn't going to work. I see it and I think, 'Wait a second. I could be on the same line tomorrow.' No way, Winston. Let's do a rethink."

Lamonte was well prepared for Spector's reaction. The day before, Lamonte told me that he goes into every meeting with two or three captions for every card, because he knows that Spector "starts freaking out" whenever something veers toward the painful reality of American life today—that people die, that they get fired, that they fall out of love, or, most important, that they don't always buy Middleton cards. So Lamonte had a fallback caption in his back pocket.

"How about if they're at the window of a travel agent instead of the unemployment line?" he asked. "The idea is that, instead of getting fired, they're using the Chrismukkah week as a way of getting a much-needed vacation. And Santa wouldn't be crying. He'd be holding a pair of plane tickets and wearing a Hawaiian shirt."

"Santa in a Hawaiian shirt! I love it," Spector said. "Remember when we did that line of winter vacation cards and had Santa in a Hawaiian shirt on the cover?

They moved like hotcakes at a Vegas buffet. We were even able to spin off the shirt! This is great. We could have a Hawaiian shirt be the symbol of the, of the . . . um, help me out here, people—"

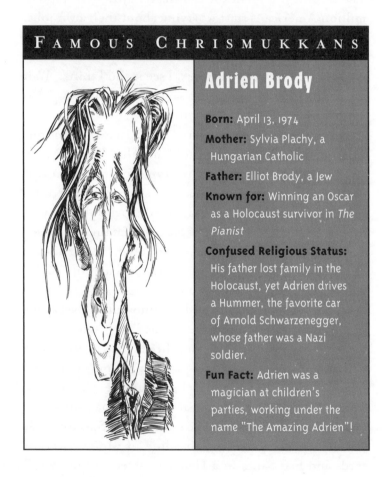

FAMOUS CHRISMUKKANS

Adrien Brody

Born: April 13, 1974

Mother: Sylvia Plachy, a Hungarian Catholic

Father: Elliot Brody, a Jew

Known for: Winning an Oscar as a Holocaust survivor in *The Pianist*

Confused Religious Status: His father lost family in the Holocaust, yet Adrien drives a Hummer, the favorite car of Arnold Schwarzenegger, whose father was a Nazi soldier.

Fun Fact: Adrien was a magician at children's parties, working under the name "The Amazing Adrien"!

"Of the carefree nature of the Chrismukkah holiday," Lamonte said.

"Exactly," said Spector. "Great work. We have a card and a shirt. This is great. OK, who's next?"

The Misunderstood Genius

As Lamonte was sitting down, Jaime Usinger started getting up and moving toward the boss. Spector had told me to watch out for Usinger, but even without the warning, I would've noticed that he stood out like a roast beef at a vegetarian wedding. Covered in tattoos and pierced from head to toe (and, presumably, some places in between too), Jaime Usinger sees himself as the company's envelope-pusher, the guy whose job it is to constantly remind Middleton that there are other markets than people over 50. Twice in the last six years, Usinger has threatened to quit the company if it didn't let him spin off his own boutique division, which he calls Punkards. Of course, the company bureaucracy has resisted and, even more predictably, Usinger has remained at the company, churning out edgy, but still decidedly mainstream, products. "You know how it is with these guys," Spector had told me in advance. "They start writing greeting cards as a side job or even a joke—

beats waiting tables, right? But then it gets so into their blood that they can't give it up. Jaime's threatened to quit twice, but he never does. This job is like his crack. He can't walk away. Hell, I haven't even had to give him a raise in the last six years—and he still cranks 'em out. Lots of home runs. Lots and lots of strikeouts."

Spector even showed me some of Usinger's Punkards prototypes. A Usinger Columbus Day card depicted the great explorer and his shipmates in full retreat back to their boats, pursued by Native Americans firing off arrows and flaming spears. Inside is Columbus's caption: "Maybe we shouldn't have come empty-handed." (Spector's reaction? "It's a great card—if you're a Native American! Do you know what our marketing people tell me? Only .015 percent of the Native American population in this country even have Middleton cards for sale on their reservations. Um, is that politically incorrect? Not all Indians live on reservations any more, do they? Well, you get the idea. Who am I going to sell an anti-Columbus Columbus Day card to?")

Another Punkard, this one for Rosh Hashanah, the Jewish New Year, was one of Usinger's home runs, though. The front of the card depicted a bunch of rabbis getting ready for a holiday celebration. Inside, the caption read, "Tonight we're gonna party like it's 5723!" (Spector told me that this card ended up being the centerpiece of Middleton's Jewish New Year collection that year, which explains why he has been willing to allow this young, edgy artist to do his thing.)

Despite some of Usinger's successes, I could tell Spector wasn't expecting much as Usinger approached him with his Chrismukkah prototype. Usinger was an artistic genius, and like any artistic genius, 90 percent of his stuff was complete garbage. But the 10 percent! Ah, that 10 percent is what had kept him gainfully employed all these years. Usinger held up the prototype. On the front was a middle-aged man, dressed in the style of an aging hippie, smoking what appeared to be an extremely large marijuana joint. Inside, the caption read, "Got Chrismukkah, dude?"

There was nervous laughter. It was clear that no one at the company, not even his fellow artists, knew how to react to a Usinger design. Stuff that initially appeared to be too irreverent for the company to ever sell—like that Fourth of July card with the Arab sheikh burning an American flag—sometimes ended up being the biggest sellers, while cards that every artist would have given his left arm to draw—like Usinger's Prostate Cancer Awareness Month card that featured a drawing of a penis blowing out the candles on his 40th birthday cake, with the caption inside reading, "Dick, it's time to get tested"—end up getting thrown out with the day's recycling. "Got Chrismukkah, dude?" was funny, no doubt, but would Spector approve?

"Next!" was all he said.

"You don't like it?" Usinger asked.

"Jaime, Jaime, Jaime. We've been through this a million times. It doesn't matter if I like it. I can't *sell* it! This company will never advocate drug abuse! I told you that when you drew that National Glaucoma Month card."

"Boss, that was medical marijuana! I was trying to make a point about compassion. I can't believe you're throwing that back at me!"

"You were advocating the consumption of illegal narcotics!"

"Yes, but for a good cause! And it's time for this company to stop ignoring Chrismukkah's hallucinogenic roots! The Biblical story of Chrismukkah is inseparable from drug use. It's time we embraced it. A card like this could bring Chrismukkah to a whole new generation!"

"Enough!" Spector finally said. "We could debate this all day, but as far as Middleton is concerned, the only green vegetable burned on Chrismukkah is broccoli rabe. Sorry, Jaime, but you know where we stand on this." Usinger grumbled as he returned to his seat. He clearly knew Spector was right but nonetheless resented whenever the company's generic sensibilities imprisoned his creative spirit.

Keepahclaus

So who's next?" Spector said again. Not a single artist budged. Finally, Dolores Rodriguez started moving toward the boss. I'd met Rodriguez earlier in the day, when Spector was introducing me to the company's

Freddie Prinze

1954–1977
Mother: Puerto Rican Catholic
Father: Hungarian Jew
Known for: Stand-up comedy/suicide
Confused Religious Status: Parents compromised and sent him to Lutheran school, but his mother secretly took him to Catholic Mass on Sundays.
Fun Fact: Freddie often referred to himself as a "Hungarican"!

veterans. She's been with Middleton for 32 years and remains the company's single most successful card designer. "I just remember all the rules that my very first boss here taught me," she told me. "Rule number 1: 'If the customer has to think about it for more than four seconds, it's a bad card.' Rule number 2: 'If *you* have to think about it for more than four minutes, it's a bad card.' And rule number 3: 'Treat everyone's holiday like it's the most important holiday in the world, even if you and I both know that it's a completely lame appropriation of some pagan ritual from thousands of years earlier.' I might be paraphrasing him, but that was the gist." She showed me some of her most popular cards over the years, but it was just a blur of Christmas trees, menorahs, jolly Santa Clauses, reindeer, and gentle winter scenes.

Given her approach to the greeting card, I wasn't expecting much from Rodriguez's Chrismukkah design, but Spector clearly was. This was his most bankable, least controversial star. His dream employee. His D-Rod. Rodriguez didn't have just one prototype to show off, either, but several. The first featured four reindeer sitting in a circle spinning a dreidel. The second was a picture of a rabbi hanging ornaments on a Christmas tree. The last was a drawing of a family sitting around a table set with day-old bialys and salty fried potatoes, with all the celebrants wearing red skullcaps trimmed in white fur. Spector, whose eyes had lit up after seeing the first two designs, looked confused.

"What's that they're wearing?" he asked.

"The hat? I call it a 'keepahclaus,'" Rodriguez said.

"Keepahclaus?! I love it! I *love* it!" Spector screamed. "You've not only created an entire line of cards, D-Rod, but you've given us another gift item!"

Even Usinger had to nod. No, there was no genius in Rodriguez's designs, but Usinger was enough of a loyal company man to see that his colleague "got it" in a way that he simply could not. Besides, he later confided in me, he really didn't think much of the Chrismukkah launch and preferred to devote his attention to his pet project: a line of condolence cards for the children of atheists. He showed me one of them, but it was immediately clear that the project still had a long way to go. On the front was a picture of a boy holding his mother's hand as they watched a casket get lowered in the ground. Outside, the caption says, "He's in a better place, dear..." Inside, the caption reads, "He's providing protein for the worms!" Another showed a priest and a few altar boys stealing the watch, cuff links, and shoes off a dead man laying out in his coffin. Inside, the priest tells one skeptical altar boy, "You don't really think we believe that crap about Heaven, do you?" Usinger admitted that it might be a few years before Middleton would let him roll out the cards, but he was optimistic that with a little editing, they could be a big seller. I told him I'd think about it and get back to him.

The Commercialization of Chrismukkah

A month later, I returned to Middleton's offices and found the entire place a beehive of Chrismukkah activity. Rodriguez's cards were in full production, joined by more than a dozen similarly themed Christian-Jewish hybrid cards. Spector was overjoyed. The company was already out there pushing the cards and the keepahclaus to stationery stores nationwide.

Spector was still months away from quietly test-marketing some of the Chrismukkah products in select cities across America, but he was so optimistic that he was even willing to take on some of the company's early critics. The Chrismukkah Defense Fund, for example, recently raised $40 million at its annual "Keep the 'Risk' in Chrismukkah" fund-raising campaign. And the Sons of Goldstein preordered 1,000 keepahclauses for a "Burn Your Keepahclaus" rally set for Chrismukkah Day: December 23, 2006. And in just the past week, leading Christian and Jewish groups had started condemning the company's commercialization of Chrismukkah as a threat not only to Chrismukkah, but, by extension, to all holiday traditions. While something like a keepahclaus is not objectionable on its face—hey, who doesn't look good in a keepahclaus?—the groups were saying that Middleton's ham-handed entry into the Chrismukkah market was nothing but a merger of Jewish and Christian symbols, devoid of any of its own historical meaning and traditions (Usinger had confided to me that he worried about the same thing). The Sons of Goldstein said that Driscoll's discovery of the ancient books of Zebulon and Rotations showed that Chrismukkah had a sacred tradition dating back at least two millennia. Yet here was Middleton trotting out a line of generic, ahistorical cards and gifts. As a result, many first-time Chrismukkah celebrants might blindly follow Middleton's suggestions, leaving Chrismukkah presents under the Chrismukkah shrubs and inside the Chrismukkah socks or lighting the Chrismukkah candelabra with offering candles. To opponents, the holiday is on shakier ground today than it was even during the Spanish Inquisition, when thousands of Chrismukkans—deemed unworthy of even being burned at the stake—were stripped naked, impaled on metal poles, and left to slow-roast in the heat (indeed, sun-dried Chrismukkan was a medieval delicacy).

But Spector couldn't have cared less.

"I saw how the Catholic League and the Union of Jewish Rabbis put out a joint press release demanding an end to 'this cultural mess,'" Spector told me, laughing. "Funny how two groups who haven't agreed on anything since the Crusades are suddenly teaming up against little ol' me! Why, because I have reindeer spinning dreidels? Because a rabbi is decorating a Christmas tree on one of our cards? You'd think they'd have better things to worry about, like, oh, I don't know, Arab terrorism. But we're going ahead with confidence. Sure, it's tough, exacting work, but when I see those smiles on those grandparents' faces, it will all be worthwhile."

Even before Spector trotted out his new cards, the critics' worst fears were already coming true. Last year, Toys 'R' Us reported that it had the lowest rate of post-Chrismukkah returns since the company started tracking the holiday in 1948. Given that returning presents is a central tenet of the holiday, many Wall Street analysts had little doubt that Chrismukkans are falling sway to the materialism of the age. And when you flip through the pages of any respectable newspaper nowadays, you can't help seeing that Chrismukkah's very identity is under attack from more than just Middleton's commercialism:

New York Times, **September 3, 2006: "Pope, Chief Rabbi in Secret Bid to Undermine Chrismukkah: Plot Centers on Better Gifts for Kids, Less Guilt." (The tabloid newspaper** *New York Post* **ran a similar story under the headline "Benedict Arnold! Traitorous Pope, Rabbi Plan Chrismukkah Crusade!")**

Los Angeles Times, October 16, 2006: "Census Bureau Reports Hispanics Now Outnumber Chrismukkans in Los Angeles."

National Enquirer, November 2, 2006: "Chrismukkah Diet Shocker! Actress Kate Capshaw Blames Hubby Steven Spielberg for Holiday Flab!"

The future of Chrismukkah is so endangered that it's no surprise that Chief Chrismukkan Dylan Smith-Steingarten recently admitted that he held a secret meeting with Nation of Islam leader Louis Farrakhan to discuss preliminary plans for a new holiday called Chrismukwanzaakah. "What's next?" asked a mocking editorial in the *Blade*, Toledo's rabidly pro-Chrismukkah newspaper. "Will we all someday be celebrating 'Chrismunavaratrikwanzaaramadanikah'?

The Politics of Chrismukkah: An Uncertain Future

Chrismukkah has become such a hot-button issue that it can provoke controversy even when it's least expected. During last year's confirmation hearings for Chief Justice John Roberts in the Senate Judiciary Committee, the judge was questioned about his opinions on the normal range of topics, such as his lukewarm support for abortion rights, his inconsistent support for affirmative action, and his level of respect for court precedents. Roberts was sailing right through the confirmation process with nary a glove mark on him when Oklahoma's junior senator, Tom Coburn, who's usually a backbencher, started grilling the unsuspecting Roberts on his views about the future of Chrismukkah. The transcript of Coburn's questioning leaves no doubt that America is deeply riven over the future of its best-loved holiday.

COBURN: Judge Roberts, are you familiar with the Supreme Court's finding in Rosenwasser-Bell v. Ashcroft from the 2002 term?

ROBERTS: I apologize, Senator, but I am not familiar with that case.

COBURN: Perhaps *this* will refresh your memory!

[COBURN PUSHES A PIECE OF PAPER INTO ROBERTS'S FACE.]

ROBERTS: Uh, no, actually it doesn't.

[TRANSCRIPT IS INTERRUPTED BY AN AUDIBLE GASP FROM THE OTHER SENATORS AND THE AUDIENCE.]

COBURN: Mr. Chairman, I would like to submit as evidence a brief written by Judge Roberts when he was a mere staff attorney in the Reagan White House. In the brief, Judge Roberts argues that Chrismukkans are not a protected class in this country and that employers can legally fire employees upon learning that they celebrate Chrismukkah. Judge Roberts, can you explain this position?

ROBERTS: Senator, I don't recall the actual details—

COBURN (angrily): Don't recall, Judge Roberts? Perhaps if I read a passage for you: "Employees who celebrate Chrismukkah are, no doubt, a drain on their employers' resources and a severe detriment to workplace productivity, first taking off for Christmas Day, then several days during Hanukkah, and then demanding another four days off for Chrismukkah. While the Administration should always defend religious freedom, one must ask whether Chrismukkans are celebrating an actual holiday or merely riding on the coattails of other, more established holidays."*Actual holiday*, Judge Roberts? How can you have written such a thing, given the High Court's earlier ruling in Harris-Schnitzelgruber v. Meese?

ROBERTS: Senator, as I recall Harris, that case focused solely on the Chrismukkans' right to consume hallucinogens—a right I fully support, by the way.

COBURN: So you favor a narrow interpretation of Harris, then? You think Chrismukkans should just be satisfied with a joint or two once a year? Don't you see Harris as a broader ruling that covers the rights of Chrismukkans beyond their homes and into the workplace and the public square?

ROBERTS: Generally speaking, yes, Senator. But I don't think Harris covers a Chrismukkan's right to multiple days off from his employer.

COBURN: And would you say the same thing right to the face of a Chrismukkan?

ROBERTS: Of course.

COBURN: Well, sir, I am a Chrismukkan!

[TRANSCRIPT IS INTERRUPTED BY AN AUDIBLE GASP FROM THE OTHER SENATORS AND THE AUDIENCE.]

ROBERTS: Then, sir, I reiterate what I just said: You do not have a right to three end-of-year holidays.

[TRANSCRIPT IS INTERRUPTED BY AN AUDIBLE GASP FROM THE OTHER SENATORS AND THE AUDIENCE.]

COBURN: How dare you, you bigot! You've done more than just lose my vote, Judge Roberts, you've lost the confidence of millions of Americans who expect justice for all—even Chrismukkans!

[TRANSCRIPT IS INTERRUPTED BY AN AUDIBLE GASP FROM THE OTHER SENATORS AND THE AUDIENCE.]

Roberts was, of course, confirmed by a wide margin, but Coburn had sent a message to the Bush Administration that any future openings on the High Court should be given to jurists with a proven tolerance to Chrismukkah. In fact, Bush's next choice, Harriet Miers, was herself a Chrismukkan who had written extensively that Americans should have the entire second half of December off. Of course, she later found Jesus and was born again, but a precedent had been set.

I asked Spector what he thought of the Coburn-Roberts exchange, thinking the raw emotions it dredged up would frighten him. But he didn't care. "Nothing sells Middleton cards like a controversy," he said. "Face it, when times get tough, you look for the comfort of the familiar. When traditions get confused, you look to something consistent. When history gets rewritten, people want the version that doesn't make them think. When people get angry, they want institutions that unite them. That's what this company is all about. That's why D-Rod is such a star here. But it's also why Jaime Usinger is so valuable. When we're doing a relaunch of a noncontroversial holiday, like New Year's Eve, there's no one better. But when we're trying to comfort all of America during troubled times, there is no one I want at that drafting table more than Dolores Rodriguez. If our Chrismukkah launch isn't the biggest thing in this company's history, I will be shocked."

Epilogue:

*Beloved Chrismukkah Songs,
Carols, and Poems*

Two thousand years of Chrismukkah celebrations have inspired many tributes to the holiday that have become so much a part of mainstream culture that even non-Chrismukkans know the words and tunes. What follows are some of the most popular odes to Chrismukkah.

'Twas the Morning of Chrismukkah

'Twas the morning of Chrismukkah when all through the house
Uncle Morty and Aunt Muffy were beginning to grouse;
Their stockings were hung near the menorah over there,
They looked forward to eating red meat with Gruyère.
The children were sleeping upstairs in their beds,
Hungry for ham latkes and shellfish on bread;
Mother wore DKNY and I my J. Crew,
As we got out of bed from a rare rendezvous,
When out on the sidewalk came such a loud noise,
I wondered aloud: The Millsteins? The McCoys?

It was a sled driven by St. Schmuel himself!
This isn't a guy who has need of an elf.
He walked over to me, I watched with wide eyes;
"I found these on sale: a new pair of Levi's."
He gave gifts to everyone in our locale,
Always proud to point out, "I got it wholesale!"
But fast as he'd come, he quickly withdrew
But not before calling those reindeer who flew:
"Now, Dasher! Now, Shlomo! Now, Prancer and Mondel!
On Comet! On Rachel! On Dancer, let's handl!* "
He looked away, so I held the pants up just for size—
What was he thinking? That I've miniscule thighs?
They would fit if I subsisted only on beets,
But he made up for the slight—look, a gift receipt!
By then he was gone, with a bagel and moo-shu,
"Happy Chrismukkah to all, the Wasps and the Jews!"

---

*Handl (Yiddish): To haggle

Oy! Tannenbaum!

Oy, Tannenbaum, Oy, Tannenbaum
You really screwed up big time
You said you had a holiday
That had no prayers, no man on sleigh
Oy, Tannenbaum, Oy, Tannenbaum
Both goys and Jews think you're slime

Oy, Tannenbaum, Oy, Tannenbaum
What could you have been thinking?
Christian and Jews will get all miffed
When you refuse to take a gift
Oy, Tannenbaum, Oy, Tannenbaum
Your head surely needs some shrinking

Paint the Walls

Paint the walls with new enamel
Fa la la la la la la la la
Roast me up a real big mammal
Fa la la la la la la la la
Put me in a room with strangers
Fa la la la la la la la la
Let's have no loose talk of mangers
Fa la la la la la la la la
Better check that age-old plumbing
Fa la la la la la la la la
'Cause Cousin Morty will be coming
Fa la la la la la la la la
This holiday will sure be jolly
Fa la la la la la la la la
Let the Christians have their holly
Fa la la la la la la la la

Chrismukkah, Chrismukkah

Rushing through the mall
To please your spoiled kids
Casts such a heavy pall
On Christians and on Yids
There's a better way
To mark this time of year
Yet not be forced to pray
Or give those gifts so dear

Chorus
Oh, Chrismukkah, Chrismukkah
A giftless holiday
We never even pray to God
We can marry if we're gay!

Chrismukkah, Chrismukkah
The best of both the worlds
No model planes for little boys
No stupid dolls for girls.

Chrismukkah Is Coming to Town

No need to watch out
No need to feel bad
Stop being devout
Stop reading those ads
Chrismukkah is coming to town

Don't chop down a tree
Or put your car in some jam
You won't bend your knee
To some God who's a sham
Chrismukkah is coming to town

Bridge
Chrismukkah's a great day
No pressure to thank God
For all the things he's done for you
Let's face it, He did squat.
So use your swear words
As much as you want
Let the bees and the birds
Guide your uncle and aunt.
Chrismukkah is coming to town.

White Chrismukkah

I'd like to see a white Chrismukkah
But global warming messed it up
Do you ever remember
Tulips in December?
Or the need to trim the shrub?

I'll never see a white Chrismukkah
But I'm not singing any blues
'Cause this holiday is jolly
Even if the air's like Bali
To be with Christians and with Jews

Chrismukkah, O Chrismukkah

Chrismukkah, O Chrismukkah
Let's measure the children
We'll play with dreidels
And talk of the Wise Men
Gather 'round, I'll tell you some things you should know
Never trust the Arabs or the damn PLO

Bridge
And while we are chewing bialys from one day ago
Six minutes we gnaw
'Cause it's Chrismukkah law
Can't Kedem make a Bordeaux?

Chrismukkah, O Chrismukkah
Jews mingle with shiksas
Other yuletide holidays
Are so petit bourgeois
Christmas and Hanukkah are just a charade
Name a single present that wasn't clichéd!

Bridge
Each winter, at this time, I'm sad for the Christians and Jews
While they all pray
I can get myself laid
On Chrismukkah, it's wrong to refuse.

Should They Know It's Chrismukkah*

It's Chrismukkah
A day not like the rest
On Chrismukkah
We don't fast or get depressed
And when we chew bialys
Or when we smoke some weed
We can all join hands together
At Chrismukkah

Now don't you pray
'Cause that's for Bible freaks
And don't you shop
At the top boutiques
'Cause Chrismukkah's a holiday
A day of mirth and cheer
Where the only thing you need to do
Is take an hour to disappear
And if you're Jew or Christian, boy
You know Chrismukkah's the best
In the North and South and even the Midwest!

And there won't be snow in Africa this Chrismukkah
Then again, there never really is
Except atop Kilimanjaro
In a painting by Van Gogh
Should they know it's Chrismukkah at all?

Here's to you—and your Western vulgarity
Here's to them—what they need is your charity
Should they know it's Chrismukkah at all?

Fruit shakes whirled
Let them know it's Chrismukkah again
Fruit shakes whirled
Let them know it's Chrismukkah again

---

*This song, written during the height of eighties-style "We Are the World" mass sing-alongs, was recorded by Michael Jackson to raise awareness for struggling Chrismukkans in Entrea, but was never released because of a copyright dispute.

Brisket Cooking in Some Bacon Fat

Brisket cooking in some bacon fat
Bubbie tries the lobster stew
Muffy puts away her Easter hat
For a kippah like a Jew

Fam'lies gather in the dining room
You won't hear words of reproach
'Cause they'll later inhale that wondrous perfume
When they pass around the roach

Bridge
We all know Santa's become obsolete
And the Jewish Hanukkah fest never could compete
I hate it when people push
To get a place near the Hanukkah bush

And so I'm offering this simple song
I won't say it's that profound
But two billion people just can't be wrong Joyous
Chrismukkah all around

We're Beginning to Talk A Lot 'Bout Chrismukkah

We're beginning to talk a lot 'bout Chrismukkah
Lance and Cousin Mo
Can't believe what they just received
A sweater with yellow sleeves
And kosher escargots

We're beginning to talk a lot 'bout Chrismukkah
Everybody knows
That Christmas is full of stress
Wrapping paper's such a mess!
It ends with lots of owes

Bridge
A plate of Idaho's best and beer in the chest
Is the wish of Tony and Saul
Wear clothes all tatty, then light up a fatty
Is the hope of Esther O'Dahl
While both sides of the family just sit around appalled

'Cause they don't know a thing 'bout Chrismukkah
No matter what we say
We know they'll be miffed
When we tell 'em, "Please, no gifts"
Reroute Santa's sleigh

The Four Days of Chrismukkah

On the first day of Chrismukkah, my true love said to me,
"Pass me a stale bialy."
On the second day of Chrismukkah, my true love said to me,
"Let's smoke some weed, and pass me a stale bialy."
On the third day of Chrismukkah, my true love said to me,

"Return those presents, let's smoke some weed, and pass me a
  stale bialy."
On the fourth day of Chrismukkah, my true love said to me,
"Measure the children, return those presents,
  let's smoke some weed, and pass me a stale bialy."